Praise for *Inter State*

"This is a must-read book, it must be read to yourself, aloud to your friends, and to strangers on the bus. José Vadi's brilliant collection *Inter State* maps internal and external geographies of California through lush description and deft analysis. From the Bay Area down through the Central Valley into SoCal, this collection showcases a voice keenly aware of how history is alive both in the landscape as well as inside his own writing body."

—SAM SAX, author of *Madness* and *Bury It*

"In this lyrical collection, ethnographer-on-a-skateboard José Vadi uses personal and family history to explore the vicissitudes of California life. *Inter State* is a soulful chronicle of precariousness in the Golden State—including farm work, tech work, homelessness, gentrification, and wildfires—that also pays homage to the familiar drives, dive bars, and skate spots that will keep its author loyal until death. A rich and moving meditation on the forces that can make us feel displaced even when we know we are at home."

—NINA RENATA ARON, author of
Good Morning, Destroyer of Men's Souls

"What a pleasure it is to trace the many histories of California as mapped by the reverent and incisive José Vadi. Whether driving through a central state valley, trudging up a San Francisco hill, dodging cops, or just making his way through a decadent museum, each of the routes he winds for us is peppered deliciously with historical, political, and familial stories all the while being driven by exquisite and generous prose. All these long and meandering sentences moving languidly like a coastline, like a famous highway, like a grape vine: rippling, bending, cascading like the landscape he is conjuring, making memorials where there are none but where there should be. The writing is candid, colorful, captivating, and just like the feeling you get when you're in California; you want to stay here, on this land and in this language forever. Vadi is the perfect Californian flâneur: well paced, inconspicuously observant, just a little bit legally high, and reporting live from his skateboard."

—LAUREN WHITEHEAD, writer, performer,
Assistant Arts Professor of Drama at
NYU Tisch School of the Arts

"I wonder if our country had more writers like José Vadi whether we'd be in quite so wretched a state as we are. With wit and rage and love in equal measures, *Inter State* is an antidote to the persistent mythology of power as character. Vadi claws elbow-deep into the soil to unearth that which has been buried, forced aside, and willfully forgotten. He speaks of family and injustice, of labor camps and tech booms, and after reading this book, it is clear that anyone who writes of California without anger is a liar. I look very forward to reading it again." —KYLE BEACHY, author of *The Slide*

"Cerebral and rich with history and sharp observation, *Inter State* is a searing love letter to California, a physical and emotional map of the places and people we call home, cities that destroy as well as nourish. With smart prose and daring form, these are perfect essays for our complicated times." —MELISSA VALENTINE, author of *The Names of All the Flowers*

Inter State

Inter
State

Essays from California

José
Vadi

Soft Skull
New York

First Soft Skull edition: 2021

Library of Congress Cataloging-in-Publication Data
Names: Vadi, José, author.
Title: Inter state : essays from California / José Vadi.
Other titles: Interstate, essays from California
Description: First Soft Skull edition. | New York, N.Y. :
Soft Skull Press, 2021.
Identifiers: LCCN 2020053321 | ISBN 9781593766955 (trade paperback)
| ISBN 9781593766962 (ebook)
Subjects: LCSH: Vadi, José. | California—Civilization—Anecdotes.
| California—Description and travel. | Mexican Americans—
California—Biography. | Working class—California—
Social conditions.
Classification: LCC F866.2 .V33 2021 | DDC 979.4—dc23
LC record available at https://lccn.loc.gov/2020053321

Cover design & Soft Skull art direction by
www.houseofthought.io
Book design by Wah-Ming Chang

Published by Soft Skull Press
1140 Broadway, Suite 706
New York, NY 10001
www.softskull.com

Printed in the United States of America
1   3   5   7   9   10   8   6   4   2

inter (*transitive verb*)
: to deposit (a dead body) in the earth or in a
tomb; bury

inter- (*prefix*)
: between : among : in the midst

(from *Merriam-Webster*)

Contents

Inter State

Inter State

In the digitized Hi8 footage, my *abuelo*'s home remains: The massive fruit tree and retaining wall dividing the backyard from the shared neighborhood rear alley. An old California farm town with mini-ditches in the middle of the alley dead-ending at the wash carrying water down from the San Gabriel Valley foothills of San Dimas Canyon, Mt. Baldy, Mt. San Antonio, and beyond, down and through the suburbs and river of the same SGV namesake somewhere near El Monte's collision with the Irwindale mineral mines and drag races, that infamous 10-605 interchange. Clipped to his white undershirt is the lavalier mic I'd just purchased at the RadioShack in a shopping center up the street that used to house a remodeled Kmart and no longer houses kids skating its loading docks before stealing rolls of film. The lavalier is plugged into the wrong part of the Hi8 camera, which had been boxed and unused for years on my dad's dresser. Thankfully the camera's built-in microphone catches Abuelo's words clearly after a brief test shot of him curiously introducing himself to the camera—"Antonio Gomez"—the expression on his face like he was hearing his name aloud for the first time.

My *abuelo* exists between my first and last names: José—which I share with my father—and Vadi, the last name of our Afro-Boricua ancestors, who took the name of their Corsican sugar-plantation landowner Vadi, erasing their indigenous name Ballé, according to my dad—José Miguel—whose first name I bear before Antonio, my mother's father. José Antonio Gomez Vadi: two patriarchs resting like gargoyles on either side of my tongue, multiple namesakes for a worldview inherited to honor and evolve.

I begin my interview. My mom sits behind me, playing translator, my original Spanish lost by kindergarten. Still, Abuelo and I have communicated through the fragmented fluency I've smoothed into proficiency. My questions are about him and his life, his origin story, those stories we've heard growing up about hopping trains as an Okie and heading west from Nebraska to California, of running away from immigration, of slowly getting the entire Gomez tribe into the states in piecemeal stages, working before settling in the towns a few miles west of where my sister and I were raised but in as seemingly distant an era as our father's childhood in East Harlem by way of Santurce, Puerto Rico. That side of the lineage, however small, benefited from my historian father's ability to remember, and research. The larger Gomez side's roots start here, with a man who wouldn't let me in the house without a clean shave and short hair, the same Abuelo who told a cousin not to come inside wearing an early-1990s hoop earring slightly dangling from his ear, because he looked like a girl. Just a handful of the residual conservative qualities reminding my generation that the generation before us did not experience such a benevolent man, while I, sitting behind the camera, exploit the benefit of the doubt incarnate that is being a grandchild, finding the answers few in our family have documented.

He sits poised in a sullied but functional white plastic chair, one of many that never went inside a neatly arranged garage, his tools along the wall framing an uncle's Honda driven almost exclusively during his bi-annual visits from Aguascalientes. A long, fold-down pool chair adorned with pillows and old shirts rests on the other side of his lemon tree, his outside napping area for the last thirty years.

He was already in his late eighties at the time of filming, and I was sober enough in my somewhat reckless twenties to know that this access, like his memory, would end sooner than later. I didn't know he had already purchased his own burial plot, right next to the one where the grandmother I barely knew had been resting since just before I turned two years old, both plots just off the main road in Rose Hills, purchased for six hundred American dollars, unfathomable now when the state's real estate economy still hits families' pocketbooks from six feet under, the cost of California soil. I didn't know sitting there, kneeling next to the makeshift tripod, that nearly four years later, I'd be sitting in that same front room of his house, watching him transition into an afterlife I don't hope to see anytime soon. His medical bracelets and wallet, his bandannas, those odd Mickey Mouse white gloves I used to hold the reins of his casket, and other ephemera are still in my possession, as I'm trying to hold on to *these* things and *this* person, and if those four years studying history in Berkeley did anything—the years he instructed me to charge *con ganas*—it was to prove the power not just of being there but of telling different stories than the supposed exalted victors of Californian land.

Toward the end of our interview, I ask Abuelo if Mexico circa 2007 will become like Colombia, with the cartels and governments in accepted collusion with U.S. aid on all sides via paramilitaries and whatnot.

"Ya es," he replies.

We both laugh slightly at this, the most progressive of comments you will find from someone who probably still disapproves of my Rage Against the Machine T-shirts I hid under hoodies on sunny days when stopping by.

He straightens up and talks to my uncle, his oldest son, and my mom, his youngest child of seven, before walking toward the alley at the end of his yard. At this point, he shuffles as he walks, using a single cane and not the two-handed walker of his later years. He guides me through each of the fruits and vegetables in harvest. A flank of nopales huddling in the corner of the cinderblock retaining wall blocking backyard from alley; the chiles by the aguacates; the yard's centerpiece, a massive orange tree that housed many a childhood play session for me and my sister, its tall branches casting shadows so big it felt like a dry-heat version of Sherwood Forest. All of this grown and maintained by him until the last year of his life.

I don't know why it took me years to digitize this tape. To see him and hear his voice again. It's still hard to drive by his former home, which was also my home. I am lucky this tape outlived my laziness, these memories I am still trying to hold while watching my *abuelo, mi chaparro,* appear on a screen before me, stooping slightly with his cane at this age, showing my uncle a particularly new harvest of tomatoes he's proud of, which, if picked and boxed, are less than a full field's row, a thimble of its lucrative worth, which doesn't matter now that the tomatoes are grown by him, for him. I take screenshots from the film to hold these moments with me wherever I go, new images of a house I visited daily, its phone number as memorized as the feel of the furniture, the smell of the varnish, the cabinets now in my sister's home in a different part of a still unfamiliar state, a state that I'd rather die in than live outside its borders. Tomatillos de Mexico greet me on sight when I reenter the backyard, filming his truck and the chair and all the small new crops he'd just reintroduced to his son, before I settle on the shot of Abuelo, finding his chair and sitting again now, his cane-assisted walk a long one for him at that stage, his eldest child and his youngest child, my mother, standing near him under his lemon trees that smelled so fresh in our hands or beneath the stickiness of our shoes as kids. They all stare back at me now, camera in hand, eye in the viewfinder, devoid of questions and shooting instead the security found within our familial silence, giving voice to these harvests, on his Californian land, to testify.

In my thirties, some family members see me as ripely capable of receiving and comprehending those lesser-known family histories: the girlfriends that existed before the *tías* that raised me, or the relatives with racist fears, worried the Mexi-Rican children of my mother and Afro-Boricua father would be some type of Bermuda Triangle–infused mestizo beasts. Between the *chisme* and the facts, I knew my grandfather picked crops as a migrant throughout California. That he'd avoided immigration by having Black and Brown allies sneak him out of bars and the like when raids were imminent. There are tales of him being tall and light-skinned enough to blend back into a reentry line after being deported. Despite the Smithsonian's impressive but inherently loose curated collection of bracero workers' names and photos, few exist of those millions of intentional ghosts like Abuelo, who headed west from Oklahoma and Nebraska to work through the dead of California's nights, wiring money to the other side of those borders that only gringos deem southern.

I knew that on much of the California-bound trail, he encountered other Okies, Brown, white, and Black alike, on their way from Barstow either down into the San Gabriel Valley, where he'd eventually settle, or across toward the Tehachapi Mountains before the Central Valley begins. These valleys are the hallowed halls of seasonal agricultural demand and systemic poverty that hasn't been paved, like everything west of Riverside all the way to the coast.

There's never been a time that I've driven through

the Central Valley without thinking, "Is this where he worked?" Those orchards, buzzing by in rows of skeletal wrath—did he rest in their shade, away from the highway? For years I thought Abuelo's work stopped at the Salinas Valley, before I heard about trips as far north as San Jose. I can't trace all the miles, but I can go to those fields that have been razed and seeded and destroyed and reirrigated and dammed and flooded and manipulated to a science so exploitative that the soil barely recognizes itself in these valleys of abundance, exportation, growth, and water—I can trace those parts of the regurgitated, re-profited California to which he contributed his labor, his blood, his life.

I fly to Burbank a day before a work conference, rent a car, and head toward one of the most well-preserved labor camps of the Dust Bowl era, Sunset Camp, in Arvin near Bakersfield, just on the other side of the Grapevine, the brutal northbound drive that's a rite of passage for any Southern Californian. I remember driving it for the first time solo when I was sixteen, visiting my sister at Cal, driving an automatic Ford Tempo that would stall at stoplights while idling but somehow got me and a friend to and from the 909 and Berkeley before it nearly exploded in Upland, my mother arriving to a southbound plume of smoke wafting over Euclid Avenue, and me smiling at the journey I didn't die on. On this trip, I decided to go around the Grapevine, through Palmdale and into that High Desert mass from Mojave to Barstow that I imagined as a kid, staring at the San Gabriel Valley's foothills and wondering what exists on the other side of the Angeles National Forest.

As the October clouds attempt to hide an uninhibited sun, the billboards advertise new solar-powered communities the farther I drive north, passing Edwards Air Force Base. A fleet of turbines from the Alta Wind Energy Center stand in formation west of Highway 14 as the once-new tract homes and permanently parked motor homes of Mojave appear to the east, extending perpendicularly from the highway. I pull off for a bottle of water in the middle of a desert I and this Jeep rental with Texas plates are not prepared for, and behind the gas station stands a local veterans hall next to a union hall that both seem empty, deserted, like a quiet trap.

On a nearby corner, a sign made of wide wooden slats screams in engraved caps, I HAVE CHOSEN YOU, AND ORDAINED YOU, THAT YE SHOULD GO AND BRING FORTH FRUIT. It faces the intersection from a barren dirt lot, where water hasn't made a street-side cameo for generations, less the miniature ocean swirling inside the plastic bottle at my feet, my hands steadying a disposable camera, snapping a picture, wondering if Abuelo passed through here and what fruit God told him to harvest on His behalf.

I head north until Highway 58 takes me west toward Bakersfield through the Tehachapis and away from the rest of the northbound path that will scale the Sierras along the California and Nevada border, up toward Manzanar, the Japanese American concentration camp, just before Bishop near Yosemite. Massive flintstone mountains soon appear, surrounding the town of Tehachapi and reminding the nearby wind turbines of a previous natural order. I wonder if this town alone could finance its budgets from commercial film permits for TV truck ads, before I glance in the rearview again at those prehistoric ridges nobody can see from Interstate 5.

It's through this passage that a promise was supposed to be kept and delivered to thousands of displaced sharecroppers, a promise communicated through leaflets and other grower-made and nationally syndicated propaganda promising work, good wages, and fields upon fields to till after the sharecroppers watched their family farms turn from cornucopias to skeletons, their families devolving just the same.

On the passenger side of the curving highway a small, older brown sign announces the upcoming historical city of Keene; a large, newer brown sign announces NATIONAL CHAVEZ CENTER at the next exit. I didn't even know one existed, let alone in a part of the state many would describe as the middle of nowhere. I immediately exit the highway and follow the handmade signs through the town of Keene down into a parking lot. Three flagpoles hoist different flags: the United States, the state of California, and the United Farm Workers, with its signature red background, white center circle, and black-bar eagle.

The grounds of Nuestra Señora Reina de La Paz, where Cesar Chavez lived and worked beginning in the early 1970s and where he died, still house the UFW's headquarters and staff members. The union purchased the former tuberculosis treatment center through a white ally in the wake of several bomb threats against the lives of Chavez and other UFW members, according to the welcome sign greeting visitors between the parking lot and the buildings. All the signs are in English and Spanish. It's sunny and cold, and I'm noticeably alone and feeling claustrophobic stuck in the middle of these mountains dividing valley from desert. A consistent drone from the trains idling at the nearby railroad comes from behind a row of Italian cypress separating the monument site from the train tracks. I debate the environmental impacts of this railroad's proximity before entering the open grounds. The sound of running water greets me, the water exiting a massive stone mural re-creating one of many UFW demonstrations, below which is a well-manicured lawn with two perpendicular tablets that I realize, getting closer, are tombstones: one for Cesar Chavez and one for his wife, Helen Fabela Chavez. There's a morbid tranquility with no other visitors around this morning, one I didn't expect would begin with graves.

I stay on the concrete instead of the grass and admire the detail of the mural and solemnity of the tombstones, names and dates only. For some reason my hands do a loose genuflection upon the shocking realization that this entire monument indeed exists; I missed the 2012 memo that President Obama had recognized La Paz as a national historic site, despite initial efforts by the conservative Congress to defeat the implementation of a Cesar Chavez Day, still not as widely recognized as Dr. Martin Luther King Jr.'s holiday.

The museum guides visitors through the best-known periods of Chavez's life in a series of photographs and installations predominantly featuring the Delano grape strike of 1965 and Chavez's eventual move, or escape, to La Paz. There's a remake of an old one-room bunkhouse the likes of which Chavez and thousands of workers like him would collapse in seasonally. I don't know how my six-foot-two-inch body would stretch inside its small box of a frame, or how my grandfather's would have either, his body just two inches shorter than mine, the two of us some of the tallest of our bloodline, two generations apart. How he'd stretch in a bunkhouse like this after picking cherries between San Jose and Santa Clara, a crop Abuelo told me he hated to work on, the pain from this elevated, thorn-ridden labor lasting for days, no matter how many bottles of rubbing alcohol he poured over his body. Chavez picked the same crops, also near San Jose.

Toward the end of the exhibit is Chavez's well-preserved office, a large space full of books and iconography, a sense of intellectual order from behind the glass. An English or Spanish button prompts a voice-over story of Chavez's labor here in La Paz, noting his lengthy phone calls and constant communication balanced with his morning hikes and meditations across the grounds. I wonder where the offices were of the other union leaders, like Dolores Huerta, cofounder of the National Farmworkers Association, which would eventually become the UFW. The projection of the UFW, and of Chavez himself, as a type of savior has always been perplexing for me, knowing that many organizations and communities—like the predominantly Filipino Agricultural Workers Organizing Committee (AWOC) founded

in Delano by Larry Itliong—were overshadowed by the
success and branding of the UFW, whose reputation has
seemingly persisted, since most of the told history ends
after the landmark 1975 California Agricultural Labor
Relations Act, a first in American history, establishing
California farmworkers' right to collective bargaining.

But recent investigations by journalist Miriam Pawel
into the UFW and its nonprofit organization shocked
activist communities after accusations of Chavez's paranoia became well documented, describing, for instance,
the purges he instated against those within and alongside
the UFW who he felt were informants or otherwise un-
trustworthy. He followed the practices of cults like Syn-
anon in using harsh verbal abuse to elicit breakdowns or
breakthroughs, depending on the perspective, and ultimately garner greater centralized control for himself and
his peers. He spoke critically, if not derogatorily, about
Mexican migrants like my great-cousins and great-
uncles who took contracts, calling them scabs, enforcing
a distinction between Mexican and Mexican American
so combatively that he, too, used the term "wetbacks"
to describe illegal migrant workers. Membership in
the UFW has faltered since the late 1980s, although the
union still holds several key contracts and represents a
small but vulnerable workforce. Yet in 2013, farmworkers for Gerawan, the state's largest producer of peaches

and stone fruits, voted against having the UFW represent them as a union. The votes, audited and released in 2018, faced waves of controversy over accusations of farmworker intimidation from both the union and the growers. Still, the saga exposed the fissures around immediate allegiance to any union or grower without the specific needs and demands of workers being met.

Still, the impact of this landmark union, its very existence, is palpable amid these arid valleys historically run by an oligarchy of growers who physically threatened the UFW during their strikes and boycotts. Throughout the lettuce strikes of the 1970s, union members were violently attacked on multiple occasions. The mural sculpture above the Chavez family's tombstones was made of stone found near Guadalajara, with five fountains honoring the UFW members who lost their lives during the movement. Four died violently at the hands of "company goons" hired by the growers. Nagi Daifallah, a Yemeni farmworker, died after being assaulted by Kern County deputy sheriff Gilbert Cooper, who struck Daifallah with a blow so hard it separated his spinal cord, according to the union. Juan de la Cruz, a former bracero from Aguascalientes, was shot and killed in 1973 near a picket line in Arvin. Rufino Contreras was shot in 1979 by the armed company foreman of a lettuce field owned by Mario Saikhon, and four years later Rene Lopez was also shot at point-blank range by hired hands on behalf of the owners of Sikkema Dairy, near Fresno. I can only imagine holding picket lines in this vast nothingness, in an era of federal COINTEL-PRO support (the FBI opened a file on Chavez as early as 1965), when ties to the city could hide whatever growers want to get away with out here in the country, where the silently acknowledged underbelly of California history lies exposed at each harvest.

Still, here at La Paz, it was nonunionized workers who built these memorial grounds in the early 2000s, a decision one then UFW member described as "complicated"; a union with decreasing membership exists amid a community's familiar, persistent need to survive.

The road barrels through the Tehachapis until the base of the Central Valley appears. Rows of green fields and orchards, the mountains receding behind me, small two-lane roads diverting the northbound Highway 58 traffic westward into town, like Comanche Road, my exit, a straight shot to Arvin. The exit conjures the song "Comanche" by Jorge Ben to my lips, and I sing as loudly as my non-Portuguese-speaking self can sing, the chorus a joyful and rambunctious *LA LA LA LA LA LA LA LA LA LA LA LA LA LA LA LA* sung against the sight of fields and the occasional oil well extracting what it can. A slower modern-day contrast to and reminder of those long, isolated shots of the fictionalized Joad family in *The Grapes of Wrath*. The actors were paired with found-on-site Okie families paid by director Elia Kazan's team to caravan with their cinematic representations, the Joads, all the way to Fresno, allegedly for solid work, this scene comprising the final shots of Kazan's Oscar-nominated and impressively shot film. Steinbeck's landmark novel concludes with a different image: a young mother nursing an old man to quell his starvation—circumventing social norms in the name of survival. Yet the movie ends with matriarch Ma Joad delivering her sermon about the proverbial People, assumedly the American people, finding a way to survive on the land. The studio asked screenwriter Steinbeck and director Kazan for something a bit more optimistic for the film's ending, given that the film itself documents the Joads' impoverished journey west, the family evading everything from scabs to cops and grower goons in between, all in the pursuit of an advertised California, anything away from the book of Revelation that propelled thousands west to unincorporated grower-controlled non-cities like so many across this massive expanse. I pass Arvin High School, where kids hold signs announcing a car wash to the infrequent local car and truck traffic, and head toward the only local landmark I know, a skate park.

Emiliano Zapata stares at me from the wall of a ha-
lal market across the street. My feet are on the coping
of the bowl occupying most of this ashtray-sized, pris-
tine skate park, a claustrophobic sort of starter park
that thankfully exists here. Three road trippers end a
warm-up session before they silently pass the skate-
park baton to the handful of Brown rollerblade locals
sitting on the one skateable hubba in the park. Now
the rollerbladers huck around the park at their leisure,
pulling out phones and beginning to film, a hierarchy
from best to aspiring to sedentary among their crew
immediately taking shape, much like among the out-
of-towners who have already left, maybe toward Visa-
lia. But I'm probably too early anyway—it's barely past
noon, the old-timers are still molding themselves into
their fold-out chairs under the shade of the biggest trees
in the park, and I'm reminded of how I always called
my friends first thing in the morning to go skate somewhere in Pomona.

Nearby, a radio plays songs and commercials in
Spanish from one of the homes across the street. A single cop car lurks in the distance (also in the shade) while
parents stroll with a handful of kids on the playgrounds
far bigger than the skate park. It's hot as hell and everything seems painted sepia with or without sunglasses
on, my eye twitching from being outside, which is sad

considering it's how I was raised. Adulthood gives you fluorescent lights and a key to your office drawer, where parts of your identity hide in secure cubicles, but I grew up like these kids, skating until my legs were numb after checking on Abuelo after school.

Walking around the actual park a bit, I wonder about my upcoming conference and how long I'll have a job in any corporate office, before staring at the small hubbas and rails again, remembering the lack of fear I had bombing the hill I grew up on every day, cutting across half of a city with over a hundred thousand residents in about twenty minutes, all the way from the spots near the hospital on the north side down Garey Avenue to Second Street. Such self-propelled crosstown traffic is nonexistent here. *This* is the spot. The high school up the street is a quick bust, same with the junior high that massive farm grower Joseph DiGiorgio built a few miles away. I imagine the locals skating here and never knowing one another's last names, just graph names and go-to tricks, like those crews that shaped me, on California land designed for kids to make their own.

I drive along Sunset Boulevard toward the camp referred to by many names—Arvin, Weedpatch, Sunset Labor Camp—one of the most notably humane camps for migrant farmworkers during the Dust Bowl, compared to the heavily policed camps owned and administered by growers who were morally against the federally regulated camps. The sun-faded wood signs extending toward the street from the camp's fence indicate that this is indeed the historical site where Dorothea Lange, John Steinbeck, and others spoke with farmworkers, documented their plight, and performed acts of immediate assistance and relief when necessary, like transferring workers to hospitals, often without the permission of privately owned grower-controlled camps.

Three historical buildings and a large marble plaque officially announce the grounds as Arvin Sunset Labor Camp. The famed community hall to my right has somehow withstood generations of storms, unwilling to meet the same fate as those faded Okie shacks almost melting into the San Joaquin Delta near Stockton. Standing in the hall's entryway, I wait for an older and a younger woman to notice me before they welcome me inside. I reintroduce myself to the older woman, whom I called the week prior, asking if she'd be there and willing to show me around. We walk slowly into the hall, where a massive open area precedes a small knee-high stage against the back wall. It's on this stage, in this room, with these original speakers that Merle Haggard and many more played, helping to create the "Bakersfield Sound," making Arvin a premier folk and country venue. The floor is so weathered because of the still-damaged roof that it can barely withstand the changing climate, just like some of the crops outside, so worn it appears suede to the eyes and the touch.

The Dust Bowl's history is spread across fold-out tables on the dance floor, the skeleton of a makeshift museum of thematic dioramas for the annual celebratory Dust Bowl Festival here in the coming days. Around the hall are reprinted screenshots of the places on the grounds where *The Grapes of Wrath* was shot: the original family tents, the outdoor dance hall, the first permanent structures, all protested by the growers. Photos of the nearby Sunset School and classrooms converted from planes, students standing on the wings for their class photos. This part of the valley is as dedicated to airfare as to agriculture via nearby Air Force bases and small country runways for dusters and growers alike, they tell me, with small planes once flying low through the Tehachapi Pass between California's valleys.

I try to envision the final Dust Bowl annual celebration, wondering if they'll have a band or even a mariachi for the occasion, but my mind drifts back to the story of how Abuelo learned who his allies were in Oklahoma: in a dance hall in a Midwest town, Abuelo danced with

the wrong white woman and was approached by several
white men ready to kill my wetback of a grandfather,
before Black Okies stepped in and one said, "You mess
with him, you mess with all of us," and the fray was
settled for the night. Similar scenes of potential dance
hall violence are given Kazan's cinematic treatment, but
not the dynamics implied and masked through the era's
black-and-white films and subsequent black and brown
faces on white actors. Would my grandfather be wel-
comed here in Weedpatch on a dance night, or would he
end up facedown in the gutters, blood flowing through
the grounds and canal all the way past Arvin to the base
of the Tejan Pass?

My guide leads the way toward the front lobby and
into an also well-preserved but weather-affected small
kitchen, maintained by volunteers, to my knowledge:
women who sweep floors and get grants to preserve
the landmark status of the historical parts of a still-
functioning labor camp quiet now in October. All of
this is on the most shoestring of budgets, with most of
the grants dedicated to preserving the physical buildings themselves. I ask them if the Kern County Museum
had offered to help with the relocation of the office and
the library, considering that several historical homes
and buildings are already installed on the museum's

expansive walking grounds north of downtown Bakersfield, and the guides responded that yes, they had asked
and the museum did offer to house the buildings, but
only if the volunteers themselves could cover the moving expenses.

We go inside what was once the office of the fictionalized Tom Collins, played by Grant Mitchell, who greeted
Henry Fonda as Tom Joad. This is one of the settings
where Fonda made his award-winning name, the literal
setting of an Academy Award–winning performance.
I ask the younger woman about DiGiorgio, the nearby
farm magnate whose unincorporated community still
has his name written on the water tower looming over
old, densely populated homes closer to Arvin, and she
replies with what her daddy apparently always told her:
DiGiorgio was a generous man who took care of his
workers. Likewise, many historical narratives are quick
to note his holiday-timed announcement to (re)build a
school in Arvin, still active today. Few note that he was
one of the first owners that the growers' unions, like the
United Farm Workers, fought against to win better contracts for workers. Yet his last name still hangs over a
town as a reminder of generosity and jobs, a narrative
bent by revisionist hands.

We walk back to the community hall, and a kid

announcing himself as a USC film student comes in
a little hot, asking immediately if he can shoot a short
film here on location, but the volunteers tell him politely to check the Kern County website to gain a permit
and then quickly go back to their seemingly increasing
to-do list for the festival, while giving me a type of ad
hoc tour, which I greatly appreciate. We discuss the official name of the camp, the places where Hoovervilles
existed along Sunset Boulevard, and the rights of the
workers then and now at the camp. Those that hav-
en't gone north to different fields and similar camps or
grower-owned housing remain here, mostly with growers' permission. Still, all residents have a hard move-out
date, or reapplication date at the least, within each block
of housing. The younger volunteer is oddly amused by
returning farmworkers' insistence on preferred rooms,
but imagine for years reapplying to the same community, where you still aren't saving enough to get one of
the next-door apartments or a low-income-housing
equivalent. Band-Aids with roofs to fill Big Ag demands.
What is the bootstrap rate of success for migrant labor
camps like these, and why does the formulation of that
question have the inquisitive dimensions of a prisoner
measuring his sentence?

We talk about the fields next door (they didn't know
what was growing there) and the types of crops most

people staying here are working on, before the older volunteer, describing a particularly brutal type of stoop labor for some deep-rooted vegetable (rutabaga?) says something about how "no white man's back can bend like that," quickly following up the pause with "and Brown man's neither," and I stand there calmly in the imaginary bridge of our silence, watching the younger woman flinch but otherwise stay out of it. The older volunteer continues, details the Mexican members now in her family by marriage, the subsequent children, and how she loves everyone dearly, something I don't doubt given the kindness I received today from her and the younger version of herself. The color of the backs, the distinction between colors, like many aspects of folklore and history, is an acquired knowledge learned from somewhere and someone, and if the Where is Here, along these roads, then maybe the instructive Who is not too far away either.

Yet the question looms: Why identify any back as white in a valley of now overwhelmingly Brown workers, generations deep? Considering the persistent knowledge of who occupies the bottom percentiles across so many economic verticals here in the Central Valley, I should have replied with the question, *When is the last time a white back bent the same as a Brown back around Weedpatch Camp?* I thank them for their time, the Brown backs, their deaths, immortalized in those five fountain heads in La Paz, stooped and burning in my eyes.

Driving the rental out of the parking lot, I head north up the main strip, Weedpatch Highway 184, through the nearby town of Lamont. The strip of stores is a familiar retail succession advertising liquor, immigration services, ceviche, and wedding licenses. The short drive to downtown Bakersfield reunites me with Highway 58 and its westbound jaunt to 99. Upon arrival, I check into the renovated historic building turned into a bougie, yuppie tourist trap where I'll lay my head for the night, where the bartender will ask me, "Oakland, and you're here?" while carding me and my gray chin beard, where I'll down the local pilsner quickly before a walk to the nearby historic Fox Theater for the screening of the latest Almodóvar film, *Julieta*.

Finding a seat in the front of the balcony, I stare at the rows of seats and imagine full houses for Fox-produced classics, new at the time, seats filled by bigwigs—like Mel Brooks, who'd later buy the Crest Theatre in Fresno—who came to town to see screener crowd reactions or find new money. Or maybe they were filled by those who went from camps to houses and to places such as these as a luxury, Brown, stooped backs often permitted to sit only in the balcony (if at all); such was the theater in Oklahoma where Abuelo would sit in the balcony with his wife and the other workers, a collection of mirrors looking down on the backs of white patrons' heads and their big screen, watched by all but for few, below.

I continue to trace Abuelo's steps after the spring thaws out the Salinas Valley, searching for something we can share here in Gonzales: the line of sight from the water tower; the view of the railroad from the fields; the signs marking the historic El Camino Real. This is where Abuelo executed graveyard irrigation shifts circa 1946, before he was deported. I'm driving in the early-morning sun, down the stretch of 101 from Salinas to King City—California's Salad Bowl—wondering if Abuelo ever had the mobility I do today: now unemployed, in a Prius, taking a weekday trip to trace the steps he wanted nobody else to find. Here the 101 requires east-west traffic to play Frogger with the highway: no traffic lights, just stop signs and an inclined cross street slowing cars as they attempt to cross. White-collar contractors with Oakleys atop shaved heads haul branded five-liter Hemis over the incline and across the highway. The railroad curves from Salinas along its namesake river, a small dried-up stream parallel to the highway with lanterns marking where El Camino Real originally dotted the landscape all the way up the Peninsula to San Francisco, an illuminated history of buggies, stagecoaches, forty-niners turned farmers, livestock and railroad barons, and speculators all the same, all heading where someone with some power decided to make a town, carved and divided from Spanish and then Mexican hands, *this land is your land* if you can afford the chance.

Despite the agricultural industry of Monterey County generating over $4 billion in revenue in 2018, a 2016 KQED report noted that the Salinas Valley is the fifth-least-affordable place to live in the country, with farmworkers the most affected. Rent is comparable to Bay Area prices, with a shred of the amenities and securities. There are over 91,000 agricultural workers in the Salinas and Pajaro Valleys, with a fraction of that number, roughly 5 percent, H-2A visa recipients. Many live in the squalor characterized in, and seemingly evolving from, Steinbeck's Depression-era text, yet even signs over park benches along the walls of the Steinbeck Center in downtown Salinas read NO OVERNIGHT CAMPING. Today in East Salinas, three farmworker families split a downtrodden one-bedroom, the tourist-industry dollars of Monterey seeming an entire country away. The California Institute for Rural Studies' 2018 action plan discovered that in the Salinas and Pajaro Valleys, an "additional 45,560 units of farmworker housing are needed to alleviate critical overcrowding." And not just for single men. The study found that nearly six thousand affordable—and permanent—farmworker housing units were necessary to meet the "overwhelming need for affordable permanent year-round family housing."

I drive past the two bars in Gonzales where I know Abuelo somehow had a beer, according to my mother, who drove through town with him a few years before he died. I drive toward the high school, which bears an eye-catching futuristic mural with some vague reference to indigenous Mexican culture, the Gonzales water tower looming over a road that divides the edge of the small town from the massive fields to whom we are all apparent guests, bearing witness. I find a brand-new city park across the street from a large field with laborers actively and steadily picking up and down the rows. The seat-belt-equipped white school buses and rows of clean portable bathrooms sit in the narrow, dirt access roads behind them, testaments to those small, safeguarded amenities the UFW and many more unions fought for on the workers' behalf, against the growers and their allies in local government. I park next to the hoops and risk the public restrooms before realizing they're the cleanest I've ever seen. Outside again, I breathe in the cool air and stare into the agricultural-meets-suburban Americana scene before me: kids being kids on the

basketball court while their parents, potentially, per-
form the labor their generation won't, many leaving the
valley and either never coming back or returning with
new innovations. Gonzales is seen as a small local model
of economic innovation, leasing new wind turbines to
Taylor Farms for revenue generation, these few but massive sentinels that can't help but loom over every part of
town. The town has sold land to weed farms and tech
firms alike, cutting through red tape like an excited
stockbroker. Who in the scene before me will become
CEOs of those new enterprises?

I head toward the turbines and the bigger fields west
of 101 along River Road, a few miles from the almost
original factory-built town of this valley, Spreckels. The
elevated view from the road allows me to see the breadth
of the Salinas Salad Bowl. I pull over at a turnout and
take it in, this part of California that has helped feed
the nation for generations, where Abuelo once worked
all night. My mind wanders, envisioning him in the
middle of a long shift, moving and reinstalling twenty-
plus-pound pipes all over the field, ensuring its health
and future profit in the dead, cold moonlight. I imagine
him smoking a joint, that sweet, racialized devil's lettuce now legalized and ready for sale, before whispering, *A la chingada*, and turning the pipes on full blast,
flooding the fields to a point of no profitable return, no

computer auto-shutting off this perfect sabotage, a cog in the wheels of an abusive industry, feeding America one unpaid worker at a time, with deportation raids conveniently executed at the ends of harvests.

The homes turned businesses along River Road offer wine tastings, vineyard tours, and wedding rental opportunities. The nicer, bigger homes on this side of town turn into gated communities the closer they are to Spreckels, the now defunct sugar beet refinery behind massive green fields. Claus Spreckels founded his town—now a census-designated city just southwest of Salinas—in 1897, launching his technologically advanced sugar beet factory in two years, with advancements in irrigation and row agriculture leading to record profits. Sugar beets are infamous for their deep roots and the physical toll they take to pick. Residents of Spreckels all worked for the refinery, with these fields yielding equal parts high demand and high turnover of seasonal workers, including John Steinbeck, who toiled in the fields and worked here in town. Steinbeck eventually worked in the Spreckels chemical labs, inspecting the quality of the refined sugar before it went to market.

Decreased domestic labor availability leads to increasing grower reliance on the H-2A visa program, which growers can only apply for if they can guarantee proper housing for the seasonal workers hired explicitly to meet seasonal demand. New grower-owned migrant-labor housing on part of the former Spreckels factory grounds has enraged the local community. Tanimura and Antle (T&A) purchased the grounds of the Spreckels Sugar Company in 1982, its website advertising an employee-owned family farm. One of the original founders, George Tanimura, and his family were victims of Japanese internment. Their iceberg lettuce business in Castroville was decimated and stolen from the family, with George interned in Arizona while his brothers fought for American forces abroad in World War II. The Salinas Rodeo Grounds near Sherwood Park may have been where they were temporarily detained, one of many county fair sites throughout the state with rock-shaped plaques now detailing the number and destinations of those interned across California, each plaque signing off with the statement "May such justice and humiliation never recur."

Hundreds of T&A workers have occupied the Spreckels Crossing housing complex annually since 2015. Nearby Foxy Produce received approval in 2016 for a similar six-hundred-worker housing complex and hired the same contractor as T&A. To the credit of the residents of Spreckels, they noted in public town hall meetings their concerns with the well-being of the farmworkers, with maintaining the quiet pace of this small town, with wanting workers to be able to work and live on the fields in some capacity, their concerns not rooted in xenophobia. These claims are tainted with a self-espoused knowledge that single men with idle hands (all the workers are presumed to be men, when in fact there are also female residents) will naturally lead to the type of drink and prostitution only white-collar executives can buy behind closed doors. There is little recognition of how the economies behind manual labor, sex work, alcohol, illicit narcotics, and even law enforcement and correctional facilities all support one another in the valley, California, everywhere, this well-oiled profitable game of Whac-A-Mole shaming many plays.

I suppose the residents and not-elected, de facto mayors of non-towns like Spreckels should be given some benefit of the doubt, compared to their peers in Nipomo, in San Luis Obispo County, who in 2016 torched multiple city-approved and city-funded housing units for seasonal H-2A recipients, the buildings' ashes like a bulldozer's teeth mashing hope to the ground. As of this writing, no arrests have been made. The residents of the city of Acampo approached a similar camp with a public-and-legal-pressure scheme mixed with pure propaganda, with one of the main organizers, Susan Aguirre, noting, as reported by the Stockton *Record*, "that because the camp will be fourteen steps from her front door, her family—particularly her teen-age daughters—will not feel safe in their own backyard for fear that strangers will be able to see them. She added because the laborers will most likely be migrant work-ers, there is no way to determine if any of them are sex offenders or pose a danger to the community."

There's a cyclical, tragic irony as grower-funded housing yet again becomes an agricultural economic necessity. Grower-controlled housing used to be the type of goon-enforced quarters that more self-regulated camps like Weedpatch aimed to correct with ameni-ties like running water, showers, toilets, and a sense of ownership and self-determination. Yet years after the Dust Bowl, in early 2018 in nearby Soledad, a contrac-tor was fined nearly two hundred thousand dollars for "inhuman" housing conditions for twenty-two summer 2017 cauliflower and lettuce workers, all of them forced to live in cramped conditions with "one shower and sink in unsanitary restrooms infested with insects. In addition, local health authorities determined the water provided to employees for drinking and washing was unsafe for human consumption."

This is what some here fear the most: someone like me standing around as a Brown solo male, taking pictures of the former Spreckels factory from across the street near the still-functioning post office, the exploratory freedom associated with boredom, and the ability to research this seemingly ghosted town. The now-acquired factory, the small-town park, and the architecture of the school make me feel less like a Molotov cocktail–throwing raconteur and more like a Reagan-era Marty McFly transported to 1955. I wouldn't be able to live here anyway without a contract with the farm, much as a bracero can't enter America without a contract with a grower, and when a town stays unincorporated and de facto mayors are cited like scripture in local news, it reminds me of how those names, the people along whoever's road, maintain their power in fear of its loss.

I drive back toward Chualar to the roadside hand-made cross I passed on the way to Gonzales. It's here, where Alta Street meets Boone, that thirty-two braceros of the more than fifty on board a bus were killed on September 17, 1963. The driver, his vision already impaired, yet hired and approved to transport human life, failed to see the oncoming Southern Pacific Railroad train, deciding to play chicken on the wrong part of the road at the end of a long workday. Considered the deadliest automobile crash in U.S. history, it sparked an outcry among activists and farmworkers alike, evidence of the malicious care given to bracero workers.

The bracero program began in 1942 as a wartime measure to meet domestic agricultural demand through a series of agreements with the Mexican government through 1964. Mexican workers, exclusively single men, separated from their families, were recruited at bracero centers throughout Mexico, promised adequate living conditions, and ensured a safe return to Mexico at the conclusion of their work contracts. The agreements didn't note that bribery was widely considered the best way to gain the best contracts, those above the thirty-cent minimum wage, nor was the celebratory DDT shower upon stateside arrival noted in the contracts, same with missing wages or unreceived paychecks, the braceros' liberties ending like a contract's term. The largest foreign worker program in U.S. history, it forever reshaped the migratory patterns of Mexicans and Mexican Americans throughout California and the Southwest; many criticize today's H-2A visa program as a diet extension of a questionable labor program.

Irapuato was a Mexican city with a huge bracero recruitment center in the state of Guanajuato. My uncle can still list off the other nearby cities where bracero workers were also courted and tells his stories about eventually living in Tecate and going to dive bars in Tijuana, only to find his car on blocks, tireless and stripped, upon exit—this is a Mexico I don't and will never know, born here and inheriting their memories. The Gomez family lived off the main road of Irapuato, and my mother was raised there until the age of seven. In the early 1950s, men strolled up and down the strip, starving, waiting on a bracero contract or eventually giving up and attempting other means to find work.

Amid the waiting, folks figured out which homes along the main road were generous with food or shelter. My uncle likes to tell the story of a man coming to their door, asking for food. First, he asks for a little bit of steak. If not steak, could they spare bread? If not bread, maybe soup. My grandmother instructed my uncle to reply, "Only rice and beans," which he repeated multiple times until the waiting bracero thanked him before turning down his offer and leaving. An example of not being truly hungry, according to my grandmother. Still, my grandmother fed many, telling workers and nearby children alike to scrape her pots, like in that scene of Ma Joad at the Weedpatch camp, telling starving Okie kids to grab a stick and eat what they can find.

I take a photo of the cross while laborers work in the field in the background across the street, those same old white school buses and portable bathrooms nearby on the cross street. There's no date for when this DIY cross was erected and no knowing how long it took for it to fall apart from weather. A plastic green produce tie connects the left side of the cross to the electrical power line pole, supporting the memorial against the wind, its Mexican and American flags heavily tattered and frayed. The top of the cross reads RIP, formatted like a staircase descending left to right until it reaches the word LOS, and the horizontal portion of the cross reads 32 BRACEROS. Small, tacked-on cardboard squares read 17 and 1963, for the day and year of the incident, the number 9, for the month, missing in action, the shadow of the cross falling in the direction of the accident's point of impact.

What would a proper bracero memorial look like, and would it be a tourist attraction? Maybe just replicate the funeral turned political shit show for those thirty-two killed braceros, which took place at Palm High School just off Main Street and behind the massive Salinas High School. A choir from a nearby Catholic church that had only recently begun accepting Mexicans into its congregation sang hymns over the thirty-two caskets in a filled gymnasium, with thousands of farmworkers outside, barred entry, while politicians observed the sorrow from inside. The caskets, laid out two by two, formed a massive cross, documented in *The Salinas Californian*, that took up the whole gym. Maybe a permanent cross instead, one hundred yards tall and wide—bigger than the one currently lurking over the football field at Ripon Christian High School just off Highway 99—with permanent American and Mexican flags hung where Jesus's hands once bled. For kicks, commission an artist to paint a big DDT spray can installation in Sherwood Park right across from the newly refurbished, massively tall public sculpture *Hat in Three Stages of Landing* by Claes Oldenburg and his wife, Coosje van Bruggen, three steel hats descending across the park from as high as eighteen feet off the ground. I can hear Abuelo, like the many Salinas residents upon the sculpture's installation in the late 1970s, criticizing the hats for not resembling Stetsons, the formed, harder-brimmed hat of cowboy and vaquero choice; instead, they're the non-Stetson droopy-billed hats falling from the Salinas rodeo stands. The DDT itself can fall on the colander-style non-Stetsons, trickling down to the grass below, like the residual poison kissing the roots of those immense, lonesome fields.

The sounds of truck and train engines haunting the cemetery are clearer than the sight of the mass grave I'm looking for at the edge of Fresno's Mountain View Cemetery. A dirt road with wooden engraved signs notes the entry points to the cemetery's small paved streets, creating a procession out of any form of traffic. The main road has signs for the adjacent school for industrial truckers, who upon course completion, become registered professional eighteen-wheel ghosts floating across this country's biggest sky in three-week increments; the sacrificial relationship

of time and commerce's demands formulates the normal
speed of "rail" that is this valley's speed. The Southern Pacific, too, is audible in every town it cuts through, not the
first or last industry to disrupt this soil, and in this soil,
those bodies who could afford it rest, their tombstones
perpendicular to the earth, casting shadows of their presence across a brittle St. Augustine.

The tombstones of the town's oldest parishioners and
priests face the crematorium and its tiled murals and
white sculptures of angels connected to the roof at their
feet, hanging above the scene. A natural V cuts through
the oldest, widest part of the grounds like a pried-open
prayer, with smaller plots dappling what space remains
on the other side of the crematorium. I can't find the
tombstone, just five years old, bearing the names of
twenty-eight previously anonymous ghosts simply known
as "Mexican nationals." What appears to be a metallic
electric generator grate is on the side closest to the fence.
I walk toward it, finding it to be instead a massive tombstone, the tangible output of a writer and a priest using
all possible funeral and Mexican government records
to identify and name those formerly anonymous bodies killed after the plane deporting them, taking them
to El Centro via Burbank, crashed into the side of the
Coalinga mountains west of I-5 on January 28, 1948.

I take a photo from the top of the grave looking east,

my back against this fence marking the end of the cemetery grounds and the start of the commercial trucking school on the other side, trying to re-create the angle of the original photo taken for *The Fresno Bee* in the early summer of 1948, of a priest and a small crowd saying grace over two neatly lined nameless caskets. The small tree to the left of the grave now hangs its shadow over those caskets resting underground, a few feet below the large slab of a new marble tombstone that lists the names of all twenty-eight killed, has biblical scripture in English and Spanish, and even depicts the image of the patron saint of farmworkers, San Isidro. A bilingual note describes how the men were killed "when a chartered immigration plane crashed and burned in Los Gatos Canyon" in what was "the worst airplane disaster in the history of the Central California Valley." Three American crew members and one immigration officer were also killed, their names also included on the tombstone, though their bodies remain in their original plots nearby. The original plaque is included at the base of the mass grave and new memorial slab: 28 MEXICAN NATIONAL CITIZENS WHO DIED IN AN AIRPLANE ACCIDENT NEAR COALINGA, CALIFORNIA ON JAN. 28, 1948. R.I.P.

Signs advertise one hundred new grave sites available for purchase, preregistration incentives included.

It's hard to imagine considering today, amid another housing crisis in California, that ten years ago, Stockton and San Bernardino went bankrupt partially due to a slew of new homes built on subprime loans. A suburban sprawl in the middle of the valley is the trend facing towns south of Fresno, like Lemoore and Hanford, with developers pitching high-speed rail to the moon in hopes of a new sell. And I imagine living here, maybe somewhere near the Thai Buddhist temple I saw on the way here, visiting Abuelo's grave—one he didn't pay for—every weekend. What if my grandfather had been deported by air instead of by train or bus in 1946? Would his fate have been as unnamed and unremarkable as that of those twenty-eight in Coalinga or as politicized as that of the thirty-two in Chualar? Maybe this explains the only wish he expressed to my mom—to die in his own home—knowing full well the dimensions of those graves at the farthest edge of a cemetery's grounds.

I stay the night in Fresno before heading south to Pomona, visiting family again while I still can. The job prospects are coming and going fluidly enough in my inbox that I don't feel bad wandering around and finding another forgotten valley theater that, unlike the Fox in Bakersfield, is still very much in prerenovation efforts.

The Crest is a dilapidated theater at the end of a downtown many hope to see booming outside of the minor league baseball season with the growth of high-speed rail. But this theater looks particularly bleak: all the windows and doors taped up with fresh tan butcher paper, a single door open, and three people waiting for clientele. With the massive downtown park and the courts and city hall nearby, I imagine during the week the businesses and streets and traffic all bustling, but who am I—some out-of-town city slicker trying to find culture by attending movies? *Back to the Future Part II* and Michael J. Fox hoverboarding against the dark, baroque, gaudy wings and oddly fake sculptures of the Crest are enough to suck in me and my five dollars, not to mention my need to walk here and rest a bit, ruminate on the casual arbitrary placement of an entire mass grave of bodies on Fresno's west side, and lurk with my fellow Friday-night Californian nerdy lurkers. The nearby Warnors Theatre is closed, and so is the Fox, I think, so with the exception of whatever small events are taking place at the nearby Selland Arena, Fresno is dead. Obviously, "dead" is a relative metropolitan term. Maybe someone's getting ready for a dirt party out the back of someone's pickup truck near Kings River, or someone's getting stoned for the first time behind some shitty fast-food chain they'll later spend the night inside until closing, or someone's questioning the sky around them wondering when they'll be old enough to buy a car, drive somewhere they actually feel at home, and never look back at the home assigned to them by geographic default. I felt that desire more than anything east of the 605; I can only imagine how big and small the sky feels here.

A couple wearing all black stereotypically takes the ravens' nest seat beneath the projector at the top of the stairs. My sour candy, soda, and I turn toward the stage, noticing the massive absence of front orchestra-level seats. Standing general admission for nobody tonight, it seems, just the mid and upper levels. I sit in the front, stage left, diving into the candy—sugar-drenched and sour-soaked—and with a single swallow of that first piece, the wrong pipe gets the wrong sweet and sour, and soon the coughing begins. A coughing that reminds me of a bout with bronchitis circa 2008, coughing until my ribs fractured. This cough projects me into the hallway for five minutes, trying to find a solution, before spiraling me downstairs through the cavernous white walls into a bathroom full of multiple broken stalls. I find the most functioning toilet stall, a shower curtain for a door, and cough my lungs into oblivion, turning my throat a dry, parched red that I find in the blood Pollocking my saliva.

I stumble back to the hotel and pass the newly installed public art displays near the minor league baseball field and the ground-broken high-speed rail station.

I wonder how many security cameras are watching me, how many cops are out at this time of night, what parts of town they go to on a Friday with as dead of a downtown as this, and arrive at the hotel designed to accommodate the convention center next door. There are groups here for a youth robotics convention, a youth mixed martial arts league, and a youth cheer or color guard competition. The parents are everywhere though, standing around, drinking beers, their voices easily carrying through the open-space layout. I find a vending machine on the fourth floor, buy every cough drop and lozenge available, and head back to my room, coughing the advertised smells of the Swiss Alps and honey and the remnants of sour candy, waking almost hourly in the corner of the bed, recounting my nightmares of every Fox Theater in California burning down, thinking of the many movies Abuelo and his compadres were never permitted to see, wondering if he'd laugh at or applaud my stupidity for thinking I could find him again somewhere between the concession stand and the image of Michael J. Fox outwitting a bunch of goons in the 1980s vision of what the twenty-first century actually looks like, Abuelo's spirit somewhere wondering how strong I could be if a *pinche* piece of candy destroys my plans, these thoughts racing along the tracks of my consciousness until I pass out again atop the sheets.

I wake up with a choke hold for a throat, trying to mouth words to myself in the morning, my car just as sluggishly backing out of the hotel parking lot, crawling toward the northbound on-ramp. Something smells like it's burning, but damn near everything does this early when the eighteen-wheelers take over both lanes, doing their slow-motion slalom routines. The car is slow to warm up, struggling to get to Madera, all to see those newly constructed pillars treading land, acquired or seized from old homes and businesses along Highway 99's eastern side. This will more or less be the top of the high-speed rail, heading just a bit farther north to Merced before barreling through Fresno to Bakersfield. The battered reflector dividers thud hard against my tires as I enter a type of neighborhood that always exists near or south of train tracks in most towns across the state—dirt yards, rusted metal fences, chickens, new truck out front, and at the end of the block, a dirt road to the northern start of holy-grail statewide transportation. I stop the car and take a photo: the still-under-construction, temporary terminus of the elevated rail line that, from my angle, is crashing into the homes next door. This neighborhood may or may not remain if this line does or does not get completed.

Driving toward the highway, I do the familiar math of how long it'll take me to get to the Grapevine, how much gas I'll burn before I have to refuel, and where within that intersection my hunger or need for a caffeine fix will kick in full throttle. I find the southbound 99 sign toward downtown Fresno, accelerate faster than usual onto the highway, and notice the cars near me quickly trailing behind. I continue mapping the drive ahead—that massive space between Fresno and Bakersfield that used to house the Tulare Lake, dried and dammed to force the valley into profitable fields—and as I look in my rearview, all the cars and trucks are noticeably decelerating behind me, a police chase without sirens where I am a fugitive from no other crime than lurking at soon-to-be train tracks, and it's then that I feel my wheel first turn into a hubcap before hearing the pop of the rear driver's-side tire exploding into oblivion. This newfound weightless space between sound and navigation under duress is a zen type of knowledge I never want to experience again at seventy-plus miles per hour. I punch the hazards while pulling this three-legged dog of a Prius over, nothing flashing before my eyes—just the immediate silence of a car going seventy on three wheels—and I manage to stop about fifty feet ahead of where the on-ramp merges with the highway, a bend in this curve I hope everyone recognizes here, this early in the morning. My mind flashes to the made-for-TV-movie scene of James Dean crashing his car where Highways 41 and 46 meet, way south of here but close to where those braceros and the American staff all died together near Coalinga; my car's passenger side is parked in a dirt shoulder filled with the kind of detritus that could puncture the other three tires. Neither James Dean's nor his companion's ghost are anywhere to be seen this high and deep in the valley.

Shaking, I call the number on the back of my AAA card. When the calm operator asks if I'm safe, I hesitate before saying yes, knowing to say a censored version of "nope" when asked if I'd like officer assistance. A tow-truck driver soon appears, a doppelganger of my cousin—all-black outfit, long shorts, goatee, Raiders hat—and he quickly tows me back toward Shaw Avenue, where we drive past the Forestiere Gardens that are still probably flooded or frozen this time of year. We talk about where I'm headed; how his recent trip to LA went smoothly with his girl and her kid; how this pickup is kind of a favor for a friend of his, a type of freelance situation. I thank him again before admitting my dumb ass was taking an off-road pic of a rail that may never exist, probably puncturing the tire somewhere between the construction site and 99. He tells me a story that I'm sure some people have around these off-ramps, about a friend of his who sold his shop—the property and the land rights—to the representatives of the California High-Speed Rail Authority after negotiating and holding out for years. "A couple of million," he says, which sounds great, *and* his friend was able to keep a smaller version of his shop nearby. But this is a rare success story, particularly in light of the governor's new announcement about limiting track construction from its northern point in Merced through the historic fields west of 46 down through Hanford and into Bakersfield, and stopping there. No more Los Angeles to the Bay via San Jose; just a high-speed rail for the very community that voted against it. "Think it'll ever get built?" I ask the driver, and he, too, doesn't think so. "A bunch of abandoned sites and relics," we say aloud, knowing those former industries discarded along 99, this lost highway where thumbs are still raised for rides along fields everyone fears losing but which most locals know are drying up from years of Big Ag bust and boom, crops, and growers' manipulation of the flow of water.

I shake hands with the driver and enter the seemingly brand-new tire store half a mile east of the highway. Inside the lobby, a home makeover show is playing on the mounted television, the contractor actively trying to flip a Chicago townhouse at a minimum value of one-point-something million dollars, and I wonder at the audacity of someone who can just come in as a buyer and say, *No,*

no, the updated plans are such and such, and then I remember Caltrans and the High-Speed Rail Authority of
today, and the Standard Oils and Southern Pacifics and
the Kerns and the Sutters that preceded them, who all
surveyed before stealing the federal land Manifest Des-
tiny rested its boots across, a corporate entitlement as
American as apple pie and the Chevrolet that paved Los
Angeles seventy years ago.

The manager—an intimidatingly handsome, older
Brown man in much better shape than me—appears
concerned. "Did you drive the car a bunch before the
flat?" he asks, and I truly don't know. But immediately
the cerebral backtracking begins, that sluggish morning commute toward the construction site, before he
describes how my tire popped in such a way that the
axle spun the shrapnel forward, directly against the fuel
line of the car, adding pressure with every yard I drove.
About a hundred yards more, he says, and the combined
pressure would have broken the fuel line. He delivers his
assessment with that concerned dad-meets-narc glance
that tells me dude is serious as hell and isn't caffeinated
enough to be so but *is* so for my vehicular edification. I
point to the tire he suggests on the list of options, sign
my name twice, say thank you, and wait. Twenty minutes and a new tire later, I'm back on 99 south, driving in
silence, listening for the heavy thud of the lane reflectors

or the sight of slowing cars far behind me, waiting for my disaster.

When Governor Gavin Newsom spoke about changes he was making to the high-speed rail, he noted that the initial segment from Merced to Bakersfield will "revitalize the state's agricultural interior" and that we shouldn't see what I saw—a ghost train in progress—but instead "it's about unlocking the enormous potential of the valley." I drive south more aware of the sense of borrowed time than ever before, and ask myself, "Who has the power to navigate California?" I immediately answer, "Nobody"—we all pay a cost whenever we decide to move anywhere within this state. It's why locals here steady their speeding trucks against moments of grotesque acceleration, to save gas. It's the privilege of my "free," jobless time to explore the official and lived histories of those before us in this state pillaged, conquered, and divided by the Civil War. If I continue to follow the clues of Abuelo's path to California, going all the way to Oklahoma and Nebraska, to as many fields between here and there that still remain, will I meet others like me, living between our known reality and the gray areas of the displaced narratives preceding us, spread across memory, oral history, burnt photos without smiles? Will we discuss our mothers' favorite bands and how their mothers, like mine, spent their paychecks on new vinyl and headphones so their parents couldn't hear the mind-bending sounds of '68; how bad our Spanish is; and how we still talk to our elders in the morning, knowing they're awake, watching? I repeat Abuelo's phone number to myself as much as his address, his final destination, or at least where I last saw him breathing, repeating the numbers and letters to myself, a history built on land he acquired.

I was standing in a California state landmark when he died—Mills Hall at Mills College in East Oakland— my father on the phone describing the scene to me of Abuelo, with his in-house hospice, meeting an extremely known fate. I was thankful for the end of his body's suffering while immediately longing for his voice, the way his jaw trembled when he laughed, the leather of his skin, and the kindness of his eyes, wondering when I'd digitize that tape. In the dead of night I want to place a plaque at his former home noting, HERE STANDS A HOME FORMERLY OWNED BY A MEXICAN NA-TIONAL, near the bed of roses my *abuela* maintained by the front window, but instead I repeat his wish—"to die in my home"—to myself, just as I remember the sound of his laugh, his posture, his feeding of the backyard blue jays and his maintenance of his crops, and the way he nicknamed me *chaparro* for being the tallest in our family. The scenes are a marathon playing in my mind like a personal memorial built of rotten beets, broken septic tanks, a border agent's slurs, and the mire of sleeping in dirt at night, this memorial standing in my mind and illuminated on every drive between the parts of California I call home. A memorial like a handmade cross for thirty-two bodies flying a hundred feet into a pool of blood, as drivers accelerate past its perpendicular stakes, toward their future, one that, for this temporarily stuck Californian, ends in flames.

Getting to Suzy's

Most Mondays, the managers with homes leave for their families around 3:30 p.m. From the deep South of Market corporate office, waves of branded backpacks emerge from converted merchant spaces, heading straight to the private parking garages downstairs and out toward the Avenues or the East Bay. Other waves migrate eastward toward the Caltrain station to head south through tech's new suburban passageway to the city, the Peninsula, and the cities of Brisbane, San Bruno, Redwood City. The CEOs are on flights or wrapping up the marathon of meetings with typewriter-active labor, the digital professionalized motions of commerce in today's Bay Area.

Hiding my eagerness to leave the office and head across town to Suzy's as soon after 5:00 p.m. as possible is difficult in an industry marketed as fluid but which is an environment where time, like work, is so malleable and remote it never ends, becoming another intrinsic limb of San Francisco's frenzied Tech Boom 3.0: the post-social, mobile, and digital-first era of limitless vacation days and constant dial-in codes. Calculated, budgeted, and NDA-signed, everything here is a cog in not just a proverbial machine but in the analytics demonstrating its ROI. My only analytics are the experiences of this timed, Monday night ritual and the duration of crossing SoMa and arriving when the bar opens promptly at 6:00 p.m.

To get to Suzy's, I map the post-work crosstown trek on the city's private and public forms of transportation— both are failures—and I'm propelled instead by foot. I'm always on foot. As the number of people living in this hive of an island city increases, so does my desire for isolation, to avoid running into wide-eyed newcomers asking for directions to bars as new as the ink on their leases. So I navigate the city's side streets, the back alleys, and the paths less traveled than those pillaged by modern forty-niners upon arrival.

Suzy's is in the TenderNob section of San Francisco, where the Tenderloin neighborhood's northernmost grime sullies the bottom of Nob Hill, a luxuriously steep climb away from Grace Cathedral, *Vertigo* shooting locations, and Powell Street tourists. My expedition begins on the border of SoMa and Potrero Hill, following the freeway overpass down 13th Street. Near the parking lots by Potrero, drug addicts are makeshift bicycle makers; a spray-painted sign reads BIKE CITY to sanction this small business of found parts.

I make it to the dispensary for two sativa pre-rolls and the week's eighth, then to the café next door, where a friend I should hate for high school drama gives me free coffees, seemingly out of attraction and guilt for past wrongs. She makes lattes with well-poured hearts that I take into alleyways, leaning between streetlights and new sidewalk planters, smoking and sipping on a block of old Victorians and the new condos they'll soon become. When I get hungry, I hit up the burger spot at the end of the alley, where a girl in a denim jacket says with a guided nod, "I like the way you smell." I know the place well enough that my phone syncs automatically to its Wi-Fi. The grown-ass man who sweeps the place gets pissed when yuppies scooter their way out of the restaurant, to-go bags in hand.

My trek heads northeast. I walk down the alleys— just before they become dead ends—between the main streets, the remaining slums, the plethora of tourists, the single-room occupants above Market, the cops in the alleyways off 5th looking for residual criminals from 6th, all while I inhale clouds of smoke chased with caffeine and exhale freely during this magic hour. I cross five-plus neighborhoods, climb hills, dodge traffic and pedestrians, elude addicts shooting up—the unhoused and untreated public addictions a visual indictment of a city amid its gold rush—and visit those who've known me as a local familiar face for ten years.

Strangers see me as a skinny, tall kid with glasses and questionable racial identity who's always turning the goddamn block into a reggae concert with those cloves or blacks or whatever the hell he's smoking. That lanky motherfucker with the weird hat and glasses—all black—with his bourgeois white-people coffees, always scowling and walking fast. Their unknown faces and names all spell the same hate, projected from my anxieties, quelled by the inhaled trees, exacerbated by caffeine, this line my mind walks as my feet steadily follow.

Microaggression is so clear and palpable these days, it's a beat for the local news. I see it daily. The revs of cars cutting off pedestrians. The electric skateboards somehow made street-legal statewide by a governor running on a progressive platform. Then Mayor Ed Lee turned a blind eye to the local rapper who called him a disgrace to Brown and yellow residents. I see the new city transplants exit discreetly marked shuttle buses in tight company T-shirts whose logos turn rainbow every June for approved Pride celebrations. They live the theory that a city's social maladies don't affect those wading prosperously through its waters, in a force field of privilege, keeping their noses and chins afloat, their devices instructing them where to drink, whom to fuck, and how to algorithmically get there. A cabbie who took me to the Ferry Building recently noted how those dependent on the unresponsive maps inside their pockets know nothing about this city. He used to drive around for hours doing research—his self-designed cabbie pedagogy—to know where to go when the traffic apocalypse hits.

And when that day hits—when all five Bay Area bridges collapse, and Pacific Gas and Electric generators are bursting on every block, sparking even more PG&E-powered wildfires—I daydream about groups of tech-savvy metropolitan conquerors in the Marina comparing their competitive options on the same XcapeApocalypse app, complaining in unison about surge rates and how their boss got the last bunker near Montalvo in the South Bay.

Without walking or even biking a familiar path—one of familiar businesses, of locals, of feeling and being a part of an actual city living and breathing its daily breaths—the city is just background scenery for rideshare-app commutes that connect work screens to screens at home. Fewer seem willing to carve ritualized paths, even if that path leads straight to debauchery.

Suzy stares at me when I walk into her bar atop Mason Street. I smile and nod, lifting the brim of my black

corduroy hat that says "rare" in Japanese so she can recognize me. "I'd ask your name but I'd probably forget it,"
she says, pouring my Stella into a chilled glass. "But I won't
forget your face—you're always so sweet playing music
on the jukebox." I wonder how many locals like me Suzy's dealt with since her arrival from South Korea in the
1980s. She got in the scene and quickly became a co-owner
of Jonell's Cocktail Lounge on Ellis and Jones, still around
today with its U-shaped bar intact, and the long-defunct
Sebastian's on Sutter and Jones, where Suzy met her husband, a local. The Tenderloin is both a time capsule and
live feed of intergenerational neglect, but Suzy's bar is close
enough to Nob Hill that the grime is out of sight, blocks
away at the bottom of the incline.

I always ask if I can play the jukebox and do so again
for tonight's set. Suzy says yes, controlling the digital
jukebox's volume with a universal remote control that
probably also controls the TVs that are always turned
off at either end of her railroad bar. Three pinball machines clutter the sometimes dance floor, at this hour a
constellation of black tables and chairs on wheels that
are barely able to roll across a thin layer of carpet. All
of this is the culmination of my patterned Mondays:
a weekly ritual of an after-work coffee, two joints, as
many cocktails, and at least twenty-five dollars on a
jukebox in a dive bar where, at 6:00 p.m., I'm the first

customer and have the whole vomit-stained-carpeted place to myself.

Over the course of these Mondays, I've witnessed Suzy cradle the heads of regulars who arrive at the bar sobbing in the wake of a parent's death. I've witnessed her enforce the sign above her bar that states her right to refuse service to anyone, tossing those who disrespect the bar or its clientele. Amid the darkness, the cash-only policy, the somewhat off-the-beaten-uphill-path location, and Suzy's welcoming but ironfisted reputation, I start selecting the night's first few songs on the jukebox, rushing to get a big batch in just in case someone comes in wishing to do the same.

I play songs that make Chicanos, old-timers, hip-hop-beat purists, ex-cons who ride on Central Valley Amtrak trains, skateboarders, and me feel at home. These are the sounds that blared from cars and amphitheaters during my mother's time in Los Angeles, and that are probably blaring out of the cars that sometimes crowd 24th and Mission on Friday nights, the lowrider shows drowning out the drone of gentrified Bernal Heights. These songs are for those Chicanos who've spawned across the Central Valley, through all of California, Arizona, and Nevada, and still tune in to listen to their ritual—*The Art Laboe Connection*—six nights a week, a show on air long enough to reflect the 1950s sound that started it. My mother's and my generation both cried to these songs with our hands on wheels, steering across Interstate 10 as we sang along, a baton-in-song passed between generations on the same highways.

Tonight's set begins with Young-Holt Unlimited's instrumental piano-solo classic "Soulful Strut," a perfect segue to my current obsession, "Crystal Blue Persuasion" by Tommy James and the Shondells of "Crimson and Clover" fame, followed by some more summer-love vibes via El Chicano's "Tell Her She's Lovely" and a deeper dive into some dance-floor heaters—Brenton Wood's "Gimme Some Kinda Sign," Jr. Walker and the All Stars' "Shotgun," and the Supremes' entire discography— chased with the Spinners' "I'll Be Around," which brings the fictional dance hall in this dark vacant bar back to a measured, coupled pace, allowing me to then bring in the funk and party tracks—Yarbrough and Peoples's "Don't Stop the Music" and RAH Band's "Messages from the Stars"—following both up with "Higher Ground" from the god himself, Stevie Wonder, and quickly cruising across Los Angeles County's freeways late at night blasting lowrider classics "I'm Your Puppet" and "Angel Baby," when I sneak a fake request-line dedication quietly to myself during the opening notes of War's "Don't Let Nobody Get You Down," a track dedicated so frequently on *The Art Laboe Connection* that the legendary DJ consolidates the requests according to the names of each detention center—Corcoran, Wasco, Folsom, Chino—and next play a trilogy of songs skaters raised on classic underground VHS skate videos can recognize—B.T. Express's "Do It ('Til Your Satisfied)," War's "Magic Mountain," and Cymande's "Brothers on the Slide"—before playing Suzy's favorite, Oakland's own Tower of Power's "You're Still a Young Man," and adding another round and more tracks to tonight's agenda.

The soul tracks engender trust between any bar stragglers and me, their self-appointed (and self-funded) selector of the evening. The soul gradually evolves into the rage and warm lust accompanying my second round: PJ Harvey, the Breeders—1990s grunge that unearths the angst brimming just under the surface most weekdays when I'm at my desk.

Suzy asks, "Do you want it louder?"

A few tracks in I say yes, needing to hear the bass that makes Zapp and Roger's "More Bounce to the Ounce" amazing. I take cell phone videos of these sets for memory's sake: a dark bar with nobody in it, me sitting in the seat—able to see anyone who enters or leaves the bar, a tip I learned while reading Malcolm X—the horizontal pan ending on the image of a neon Budweiser sign reflected in a Trumer Pilsner–branded mirror, a turned-off

Pac-Man floor console, and the digital jukebox, lined in studded neon pink lights. I nurse my drinks according to the length of the set list, closing with something I can remember as my cue to leave. When James Brown comes on, the show's over, the set ending with "The Payback," giving me enough time to enjoy the song through the walls of the restroom and to say "Peace" to Suzy.

I can only do this on Mondays. Tuesday's bartender front-loads the jukebox with long, predictable indie rock songs that pass the time but fail to tell the night's story, fail to reflect a mood—his, the city's—and instead use sonic filler to leave us, the bar's clientele, subject to the banality of eight-minute art pieces by formulaic jam-rock bands. He voluntarily plays Weezer songs in 2016—publicly. Meanwhile, I sulk with a grin on these Tuesdays and other off-nights, devoid of the sonic control Suzy provides me on Mondays and of the fleeting satisfaction of having crossed a whole city trying to control something—anything—amid an untamable metropolis.

On my third (or fourth?) round of Jameson, Suzy walks over to my table. She extends her hand with an avocado in her palm, says, "Take one home." I thank her, placing it on my hat resting on the table with my drink, and I think of the way my grandfather would pronounce "aguacate."

Sunny Ozuna's "Smile Now, Cry Later" plays as

loudly as those first sung notes were originally intended. Nobody here knows how good Sunny Ozuna sounds outside on a sunny day at Echo Park or somewhere in a park in Santa Ana in 1991 celebrating my uncle's sixtieth birthday, when I first saw my cousins brown-bagging brews and realized not everyone's home had more books than places to chill beer. And then, staring at the avocado, I think of my white Californian girlfriend and how she'll be thrilled, and of those of Suzy's generation, in the Tenderloin of the 1980s, for whom the city offered labor and community and the opportunity to shape both on their own terms.

Some nights I measure the coincidence of full-time employment, the impulse to destroy myself, and a desire to escape by the numbers of songs, hours, and drinks I allow myself to consume, wondering if the regulars see another amateur barfly Bukowski, a Vonnegut worshipper-in-progress, ready to drop back into a routine of permitted cheat days and "getting a run in" on the way to BART or a few lapped miles around South Park to crystallize my new big idea turned app turned TED talk. They forget that every physical body in this city is as haunted a home as these flipped Victorians and displaced SROs, this ritual of drinks and tunes a type of aural connective tissue to the laughs and daps thousands of miles away or six feet under now, worrying how quickly such weekly sonic practices can turn into addictions. Into liquor. Into jukeboxes that aren't mine, on stolen land that the Central Valley growers living in Nob Hill have owned since the years my grandfather was still picking fields for an under-the-table existence. Maybe it's a partial reclamation of space just as much as Suzy's name on the deed or the bar's glowing sign, its decaying white-to-yellow grin welcoming mine just the same from the corner outside.

Really, this ritual ends with the need to head home. To the East Bay. Back to Oakland, a city that calls itself "the Town," knowing the many terms that city heads sleeping between the Golden Gate and Treasure Island have for that other side. There, Lake Merritt turns into a protest every Sunday, conga drums and Brown and Black people alike amplifying the soul of songs threatened in the wake of newly arrived gentry's noise complaints, another reason to put on just three more songs tonight, I tell myself in the ice cube's reflection, that much more of the songs, the voices, that raised us occupying the city skies.

This real life of cityscapes and sidewalks can engage, ignore, or destroy you at a moment's notice. Monthly checks keep roofs over our heads, this tithe we all pay to sleep close to our ghosts—these memories of friends and places and co-conspirators—who once lived here with me, at the end of one of this city's many small nooks and cross streets. On Mondays these ghosts appear, ready now to buy me coping mechanisms in forty-ounce doses after quitting my hourly work registering rich kids for private swim classes off the 1-California.

It's for these ghosts of fellow metropolitans long since gone that I choose Jimi Hendrix's "Purple Haze" as the last song of this set, his same kiss to the sky made tonight by me and my ghosts, those spirits expelled now into the night from my lungs, into the sky we all once inhaled.

Standing in
the Shadows of Brands

San Francisco at Dawn

Mari and I got day jobs at the literary nonprofits that
kept us on their payrolls through 2012 while we earned
MFAs. Framed paper in hand, we returned to full-time
work funded by shoestring grants to manage arts-
education programs with equally vulnerable funding,
scaling the horizontal hierarchies of the not-for-profit
economy.

Weekly we'd meet for coffee on the steps of the 1390
Market Street building, a huge gray high-rise of apartments and offices, with a token Starbucks downstairs
filling out the triangular block, its hypotenuse jutting
north into the Tenderloin District. Discussing writing,
our bosses, and *what we really want to do*, vague-to-
serious outlines turned our conversations into those
types of extended exquisite corpses that sharpen our wit

and fortify what resolve remains on a random workweek afternoon.

Across the street: the then-mysterious offices of Twitter, a blue corporate bird marquee telling time for the Civic Center populace. On the other side of the cross street, the rumblings of a new high-rise: an odd obsidian architectural thesis, casting a larger and larger shadow over me and Mari sitting across the street. They named the building the NEMA—all caps—luxury condos and apartments. "We're gonna sit here and watch NEMA grow up," Mari said, astonished by how fast and high the development grew before our eyes.

In the post-recession recovery programs the city underwent at the top of the decade, all we saw were cranes foretelling a future many here were not invited to inhabit. Indeed, the city's skyline was becoming the interstitial shots of Godard's *Two or Three Things I Know About Her.* "Never seen it," Mari said when I referenced it, and I tell her instead about the white stone block of a handrail leading out of the nearby building's door, how skateboarding innovator, artist, and former San Francisco resident Mark Gonzales used it for landmark achievements in "street style" and how it's still sessioned today, the new construction a steady drum of sonic racket across a beautiful art deco preservation site turned tech office, rooftop couches and the like to boot, a comfort desired but so out of reach here, bay of Indian blood and forty-niner promise.

The other night I realized both of the cities I call home—Pomona and Oakland, California—have a Fox Theater. Produced by the film company of the same name, its chain of theaters grew nationwide during the 1920s and 1930s, overwhelmingly so in California. A few searches later and I realize that the site where Mari and I met for breaks was once the location of San Francisco's own short-lived but truly ambitious Fox Theatre.

Just down the street from the still-standing Orpheum and Warfield Theatres, San Francisco's Fox opened in 1929, encompassing an entire triangular block, for a Dean Martin and Jerry Lewis concert. The theater's massively high arches, chandeliers, multilevel double-winged staircases, and a stage that accommodated both live performances and film presentations, an advancement for its time, created an overhead that far exceeded the investors' and promoters' pockets. I imagine that Hollywood celebrities could potentially catch an aquatic show at Sutro Baths in the morning and a show at the Fox at night, some classic San Francisco venues gone by the time Haight Street became America's definition of the city by the bay. Despite solid attendance for the 4,651-seat theater, financial mismanagement bled dry any hope for profits, making San Francisco's Fox, the largest west of Chicago, one of the shortest lived of its generation.

And what of two artists from two different states who both now share the Oakland-to-SF work commutes, who cover each other's tabs with money found in the back of taxis, who hold each other up while getting a future regret's phone number with the other hand, all home in Oakland where we wanted to run to in those moments, drinking sugary crap from a chain we despise in a city we tolerate and enjoy but always feel inside of and not a part of? The looks I get in some parts of town and the times she's been asked if her hair's real and I've been asked *Do you work here?*—would that still be the case, if not worse, if we were the help working around the velvet-draped Fox lobby, looking like the young photos of our grandparents in their early twenties? Would Abuelo or Mari's grandmother even be allowed into the building?

When a city's populace is wiped of its longtime residents, so goes the collective memory of this city, replaced instead with a victor's pen stroke's spoils, romanticizing the city's history away. Haight Street's advertised freedoms. Journey sing-alongs at Giants games. New and dull murals all over the East Bay—WELCOME TO TELEGRAPH! ROCKRIDGE! TEMESCAL! they exclaim—guiding newcomers through gentrification.

Sitting there with Mari, I wondered what would survive this city—new buildings, new people, or neither?—until I realize Mari's doing this thing where her body tightens into a ball before she exhales, says, "I gotta go back; bye, friend," and we part until next time, when a new floor will be finished across the street.

A new job, a new commute, and a new entry point into San Francisco—SoMa at dawn—hit me in 2015. I started taking photos of a city as it wakes.

Most of the developed photos are black blobs of dead

flash or overexposed light amid city darkness. Poor attempts and pricey learning curves that still support the timeless business that develops these errors, probably smirking like, *This kid* . . . when, in reality, I'm thirty-two and just trying to remember the late teens that felt like childhood. But at least there are photos now.

I play stereotypical poet and move shit around like tarot cards that mean more through implication than ritualized pattern. Scratch that: I shake off cynicism to try and see why the fuck I took these photos to begin with, and why I woke up so damn early: who to see, what to avoid, or what to see and who to avoid, in a city still anonymous to those in the know, and experience defines the know.

Speaking of dark photos, two poised next to each other: A photo of a friend taken in a dark bar and only three small volcano lights appear somewhere assumedly above, in a den made to inhabit our collective inferno below. And the other photo: the silhouette of what was once a strand of large braided ropes, python thick, mingling and dangling from the northernmost stairwell wall of the Embarcadero BART, the stairs I climb two steps at a time to let the dude ahead of me know that the dude behind me is walking two too, *So hoof it!* my body screams early. One guy perfectly times when he awakes from his suburb-to-city slumber to ensure that he is the

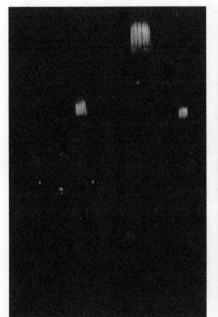 

first person out of the lead car of that 6:19 a.m. SF-bound train. If I took the liberty to beat him to the punch, oh man, my ankles would probably still be suffering PTSD from the threat of his toes, covered in those quasi hiking boots that seemingly only white straight men in business consider casual.

Everyone is trying to occupy or temporarily own vital forms of previously public space during these morning hours. Rush hour gets all the credit because everyone's awake to see it. But the lead car of the 6:19 a.m. train to

SFO is a classroom that reassigns itself to the same seating chart of public transportation each morning: The suburban commuters whose previous generations fueled the white flight to the suburbs, which is now occurring in reverse, powered either way by BART. The brunette with a full-body puffy jacket and coiffed bangs. The aforementioned balding banker with branded everything who always needs to exit first. The security guard who exits promptly at 19th Street Oakland, even though his shirt clearly says he works in Berkeley.

The second and newer train, Montgomery-bound,

is a bandage for the doubling of the population. Public transportation usage has been documented by KQED to have peaked just in this handful of years, thanks to a resurgence of new tech money, a housing price boom, and the jobs to fuel it all. Indeed the Bay Area's demographics have been altered mightily and rapidly. A schoolteacher in the city today can't afford to live within its limits. The African American population has dwindled dramatically, with the Latino and Asian populations quickly following suit. The cost of living is so high that the middle class is eroding under its weight. White flight in reverse is leading to a familial type of reconquest of the city, strollers now pushed in parts of town where previously only crushed needles found homes. And amid the pros and cons of all the changes are those pockets of space and time where these arguments stand still for a bit, hanging in the gallery of the city's waking mind, before the city finds such silence uncomfortable, deciding instead to trounce itself in its daily chaos.

And it's within this time that I arrive in the city on the Montgomery train, which turns around immediately in the Financial District to bring in more commuters from the East Bay, before I transfer to MUNI. A kid on the outbound L looks like Kurt Cobain's lost roadie: all middle-part bleached hair with black roots, a kinda chubby kid who I imagine misspelled "Fender Strat" on his Christmas list months earlier. One day he rocked the Morton Salt Jawbreaker shirt on his way to school in 2016, the band having disbanded years before.

Exit Van Ness just before 7:00 a.m., the station's southeast escalator rising toward the ATM security guards at the Bank of America on Market and 11th, a guard usually on either side of each machine. I light up by the former newsstands removed by the sidewalk trees' obese roots tearing up the corner. Walking south on 11th, nods and daps to the Brown men guarding the parking garage housing Teslas. On pace with the theater that is our lives, the northbound 49 passes me just as I arrive at the bus stop on Howard. Left turn down Folsom to a café toward 10th, and while crossing, I look down Folsom: its empty horizon, its flat accessible beauty, the flying pink pig attached to one of the nearby haunts, 13th Street and the mountains housing Twin Peaks in the distance, the quiet of a city voguing its defected seams.

Reset with three new photos:

Top left: what was once the convention center, 888 Brannan, now Airbnb HQ, and the developing city-block stretch of condos across the street, taken on the way to my tech job a block away.

Top right: one of the infamous Division Street offshoot encampments underneath the 101 and 280

freeways, belongings stuffed between the supporting
pillars, concrete planter, and the fence dividing the sidewalk from a pay-to-park lot.

Bottom: a billboard local weeklies have described as
a *fortuitous portal to Bay Area life*, posted and tagged
on Folsom and 9th, that starts with IT'S YOUR TOWN
and is consumed by the shitty two-color bubble tag. Its
audience: bridge-bound city dwellers.

I play three-card monte with this trinity of photos
for a bit, turning them into a bootleg panoramic image,

a landscape triptych of urban gentrification, from commercial declaration and coffee-thermos commutes to new condos next to new money. I wonder if these three photos can become a carousel panorama visible in an analog slide projector handheld or VR headset, whatever compels something with a pulse to give a shit and shut up and maybe even do something about the It we all try and try and try and try . . .

Do vacations reach the parts of Market Street that dole over-the-counter remedies to alley-therapy addicts in the SROs and shelters around town?

The graveyard-shift Walgreens cashier and security guard discuss the torn bar codes and security tapes found discarded around the store by some Market Street hustler who always wants to return a pair of speakers, a reminder that the simplest, most innocent joys—music being played on the streets, in the parks, by men and women not prone to return an AUX-cord-included

handheld speaker from a drugstore—are the most pro-
hibited in cities like Mayor Ed Lee's. Days after over-
hearing this conversation, I'd read in the *Chronicle* that
two workers from that same Walgreens survived a stab-
bing after trying to stop a shoplifter. This proximity to
palpable chaos is part of the everyday, even in the way
we access public transportation now in the wake of the
area's population boom.

Past and present side by side: Photos of Oakland in
the early 2000s, of pimps still buying gators on Broadway, standing proud on 14th, knowing who they are,

rooted in the Town. And last year, along Division Street, an unknown finger etched the words I DON'T WANNA BE AFRAID ANYMORE in such perfect lettering, I wonder if it was out of desperation or staged for the 'Gram.

In the silence of morning, the shutter goes *click* and no bird startles from the sound, there's merely a level of light circulating through lens and film toward the next available slot for documentation, in the palm of my steady hand. I do this carefully, walking gingerly away from each scene and moment, keeping the memory present, living past our interaction.

Mari moved out of the Bay Area in 2013, never seeing the completion of the NEMA. Brooklyn, then Lansing, and soon Lexington, Kentucky, has been her path, while I have remained in Oakland, working in San Francisco. Hustling nonprofit day jobs, writing her first book, and living off her advance, Mari asks, "How does the building look? Does it cast a shadow over the steps? Are the steps still there?" And I reply, "tall," "yes," and "I don't know for how long."

Last year an e-sports gym opened next to my and Mari's break spot, right where the line for the former Fox would have bent northwest around the block toward Van Ness. Classic venues like the Fox pale in comparison to today's optimized San Francisco, where the Moscone Center expands every year south of Market to accommodate an endless cycle of professional conferences, new pedestrian bridges span Howard Street, and hotels are booked year-round, while homelessness somehow increases from epidemic levels year over year. Salesforce rebuilt the San Francisco Transbay Terminal in its name to also facilitate the construction of its three (and counting) towers, reconfiguring the city's skyline. The terrace on the roof has ideal views of the logos facing the park from the tech and finance skyscraper offices next door, the scene akin to SimCity's logical apocalyptic end. Almost karmically, a worker caught two cracks in the new terminal's supportive beams within weeks of opening in October 2018, closing the entire facility immediately and putting the city's fate, with connecting Amtrak, Greyhound, and high-speed rail lines, in still-undetermined jeopardy.

It didn't matter for my commute though. I was laid off by year's end between the San Jose and San Francisco holiday parties so that, I suppose, the news could be a wake-up call or a catalyst to get smashed on the company's dime. After numerous non-coffee-drinking coffee meetings, I took my severance before figuring out a contract gig months later with the very company that let me go—a growing trend in tech where nearly half of a multibillion-dollar company's staff are hourly hires with limited health care and no equity.

Being a contractor is a physicalized form of second-class professional citizenship. For whatever reason (and despite petition), I was denied the traditional access badge that would allow me to move in, out of, and between buildings without escort. No keys here, just magic wands hanging around belt buckles from home to office, an adult-scout merit badge many wear to and from work on BART that says, *I am not dependent on someone else's movement to define my next step.* I wanted to ask every member of the security staff, the most diverse department—that is, if the company defines them as full-time staff—*Don't you remember me? The only non-Asian Brown dude in here?* before remembering they're as contracted, powerless, and disposable as I am, our silence in the lobby while waiting for my escort acknowledging the familiar arbitrary parameters of power.

I revisit old haunts after work along Folsom, inquiring about businesses new and gone. The erotic bakery next to Diana's Market is still kitty-corner from the Out of the Closet on 9th. A sole Victorian stands on a city block devoured by pits and massive condos across from the SF Eagle on 12th. Across from a coffee shop near 8th, two bros making plumes of tobacco-vape smoke tell me the foundry next to their robotics office "was just a satellite" and was moving back to its mothership of labor, somewhere not in the makers district of SoMa. I head up 11th toward Howard and see a new two-story corner office being cleared and converted to house nothing but a really nice marble reception desk and an even gaudier chandelier. An undergraduate with a clipboard and an unintentionally messy-jeans style looks confused when I ask him if this space will be open to the public. He asks for clarification and I say, "Like someone like me, coming off the street—would I be able to come in here?" to which he quickly replies, with newfound clarity, "Oh no—it's private." On this seven-by-seven-mile over-picked rock of gold, space is swallowed by hands stained with platinum.

The walls along Market go higher and higher, casting shadows over us all as a new business plays some song about sun and brightness and shining days and that California soul we, too, long to grasp, again. And there are no photos for those moments now gone: Two writers talking shit in the dead of afternoon promising the dawn of whatever night bears. Two souls talking shit in the ubiquitous shadows of an investment group's skyscraper.

I develop the photos in the Castro, getting doubles to use as postcards to send to Mari and other friends now gone from here. In the grid at the top of each roll are thumbnails of the successes and failures of disposable-camera photography. And when the clerk asks, "What are you taking pictures of?" I realize that without any humans in the photo, the clerk can never ask *Who*—so few humans in my photos of a city whose ghosts are still invisible, no matter how bright and artificial the flash.

A California Inquiry

(or California in Flames)

I'm searching for the way to my friends' graves by heart, by memory of their funeral routes, with the same ease with which I drive across California to my sister's house on the other side of the Grapevine. In Puerto Rico, my father's side of the family is stacked and covered by plywood within a tomb hopefully still six feet deep after Hurricane Irma. My mother's side, the Mexican side I grew up with, is buried off the 605 in Rose Hills—my grandfather and grandmother beside each other, two friends up the hill. Death articulates a connection to soil and roots, however decayed. I'm obviously and painfully soft compared to my former self, everything I'd hate myself for being. I'm searching for the mischief that was critical for me, once a straight-edge and studious teenager in a strict Brown liberal home, dedicated to living, writing "CARPE DIEM" in Wite-Out on my skateboard's grip tape, dedicated to touring bands, wondering where they were playing next (Hollywood? Portland? SF?), and dreaming, too, of the ability to move freely, to move out, to move north. I fear time is becoming the accelerated inverse of a Polaroid's development, stretched into nonexistence.

I fear losing California. I already lost both my grandfather and, per his request, his home in La Verne, the home I walked to daily until the age of seventeen, sold to a family who felt an old, well-maintained orange tree, one whose shade was cast so wide and dark it defined the first caverns of my nascent definitions of fear, was worth chopping down to afford them the luxury of nothingness, a bigger backyard, and market-bought citrus. So, too, are the chiles gone, the tomatoes, the lemons, the aguacates, the nopales, and most notably, the stretched-out plastic lawn chairs topped with repurposed cushions, where Abuelo would lie beneath any number of trees in quiet safety east of the Los Angeles people only visited for county paperwork and Lakers championship parades.

I can't go to that house now. I can't even drive by that stretch of Bonita Avenue anymore. Too angrily, too instinctually do I want to open the white wood side fence and reclaim his home, barging in past the large bushels of flowers with bees the size of my fist when I was a child, near one of two porch entrances, if either still exists, if there's even grass in that backyard, let alone the border of red bricks undulating like a million camels' backs, the same bricks I broke my first bones against as a kindergartener. All such domestic items are considered luxuries now in our changing state, replaced with drought, pebbled yards, gaudy inoperative fountains, and inflated Santas.

Instead of breaking and entering, I head toward the town center while there for a holiday. Last time I went to Miss Donuts, or what I thought was Miss Donuts, it was on 3rd and Bonita Avenue by my grandfather's house and the local but private university. Traditionally owned by an Asian American family known for their kindness and amazing baked goods, that day it was operated by disgruntled young teenage girls and the young boxer stains attempting to flirt with them, drinking coffee with a shit ton of sweetener, parodies of the hetero male stereotypes—a cop, a construction worker, a father—that defined their world view as small as this town. I realized, walking around while waiting for an oil change at a place that knows my family by name— "You're so-and-so's son" status—that the original Miss Donuts had moved near the old Super Duper Video and the even older Lucky's, both now vacant and located off of Foothill Boulevard, part of the famed Route 66, where White Avenue becomes Fruit Street. The donuts were perfect, the old war veterans perched themselves in the back with their chests facing everyone who entered, all while the family worked and chatted behind the counter. The real confirmation of this place being the donut shop of my youth was the small, plastic, jug-style cartons of regular and chocolate milk, with twist-off ties on a plastic cap. I've only seen them, in both small and large sizes, in spots like these. I buy a donut and a water, and the man behind the counter says, "It's good seeing you again," and I can't remember the moment, but he's familiar enough that I say, "Likewise."

Who lives in California with these types of trite childhood stories of watching life pass from the back seats of cars, marking time by how their line of sight changes from the bottom to the top of the window?

The question hints at the accusation: California is a destination, not a process of individual and communal survival, the past, present, and future embodied in one massive Jesus-blessed swath of western land. Future "from Californians" will know nothing about the generations that molded the state's 1950s surfer stereotypes, it's '60s heyday, its '70s resistance and challenges, its '80s suburbia, its riots and smog alerts and blackouts culminating in the '90s, the history of corruption behind the freeways of Los Angeles County or the history of water rights from Sacramento to the south. I fear we will become sort of modern-day Okies, displaced as alumni of the state to other cities in other states feeling the economic and demographic ripples of the tectonic shifts occurring in San Francisco. And those new Californians, those riding in strollers now, the unfortunate, reluctant mascots of gentrification, will they know about us, these faces their parents first saw when they entered this new land, learning the ropes of a place many fantasize about but few experience, this disjointed mosaic of a state, California?

Leave it to this Los Angeles native to assume the performance of *The Nutcracker* was, indeed, a performance— actors, characters, plots, all of which articulate the articulated—but no, the realization that this show before me was a dialogue-less ballet came after I finally looked at the playbill during the San Francisco Ballet's second dance of the annual performance, which originally premiered for American audiences here at San Francisco's War Memorial Opera House in 1944. The back of this evening's playbill notes the mayor as Ed Lee, eight days after Lee collapsed at a Glen Park grocery, a heart attack abruptly ending his life at sixty-five. London Breed, the city's interim mayor, is nowhere in tonight's remarks. The insanely impressive set design showcases massive Christmas trees littered with presents and an unspoken ritual of gift giving, appreciation, dancing, and the like. Pacific Heights is depicted onstage, providing a backdrop for the ballet dancers, their tall and beautiful statures reflected against the orange glow of a pink-hued sky. It all serves as an additional reminder that such lavish scenes and pleasantries and "help" meandering among the residents could happen, both in 1944 and 2017, only in the same affluent neighborhoods of San Francisco. Our new and longtime homeowner friends change the subject when the topics of mortgages and who bought what house recently arise in conversation, offering a conciliatory *It'll work out* or *You'll find something* to me and my girlfriend—who loves *The Nutcracker* and for whom, like for me, California is the intrinsically native and maturely desired center of our worldview. For whatever a declaration is worth: I don't want to die anywhere else.

I wonder how many ticket holders actually live in the city. I asked myself the same question a few days earlier, when we saw the San Francisco Symphony play on its home court, in Davies Symphony Hall, a live performance turned revenue generator: a live soundtrack of the 1990 holiday film classic *Home Alone*. A friend of a friend plays in the symphony and noted that though it is the group's least favorite type of gig to play, it pays the bills and engages new audiences the symphony would otherwise not see walk through its doors on Grove and Van Ness. Yet in the Davies crowd, as well as at *The Nutcracker*, there was a particular older type of white Bay Area resident. I never see these parents or their children downtown, in SoMa, or even in the Financial District: they appear from Marin County, from Daly City, from St. Francis Wood, from the Taraval and appear at the events that define the city's history and that are the first things included on any of the city's advertised fares of amusement and things to do. Women in full stilettos and dresses dine in the downstairs reception area, making a catwalk out of one the city's most family-sanctioned events, which is great and fine but just surprising how special and entertained we all must feel at the slightest possibility of being seen.

At intermission, the family behind me talks to one another across the seats. The son asks the father to confirm an argument he previously made to another sibling: that good mariachi music is solely determined by the sense of entertainment created for the audience members, and thus a mariachi group is indistinguishable from another outfit since either's sole purpose is to entertain. Absolutely right, the father confirmed, and loudly and not so passive-aggressively I commented, "Wow, I'm so happy that histories of mariachi culture and tradition and the economic survival underlying the practice can be so whittled down so as to only be part of the larger service industry reluctantly dominated by Brown hands and bodies"—I said it loudly to my girlfriend as she shot daggers from behind eyes created by two white professionals who met helping organize Brown California farmworkers twenty years after my grandfather picked from those same fields to support his family.

The movie *Coco*, the highest-grossing film of 2017, features, for the first time, an animated mariachi hero immersed in traditional Mexican culture, or at least informed depictions thereof. I saw an exclusive premiere of it at Pixar's studios in Emeryville through a friend at work. The UC Berkeley mariachi performed, as did other community groups. The codirector, who also cowrote the script and the score of the film, discussed the precise methods used to make the hands of the mariachi characters accurately depict the actual chords played. And to think that the precision and attention to cultural detail that was obviously watched by so many people still does not trickle down to the father who agrees with his son that mariachi is as much a service industry as cleaning houses and toilets.

And what of my access to either event, to have the extracurricular time and disposable income to bear witness to both a studio's sneak peek with proper cultural undertones and a city's most historic tradition? When I was a tech worker in 2017's boom economy of start-ups and acquisition-heavy old-timers, I could afford good seats to the same type of entertainment as local home-owners but did not have the ability to buy land in the state of my birth, in the state where my grandfather was a migrant, where I have taught and contributed and vol-unteered, on soil that I know first as a pedestrian rather than as a taxi fare. This is what it is to perpetually feel displaced and privileged at the same time in twenty-first-century California.

My girlfriend and I drive up the 405 toward Beverly Hills to attend a function at the former estate of a Hollywood silent-film actor, now owned by a fundraiser for the Demo-cratic Party. The cause in question—skate parks—is some-thing rare to be discussed in these environs, where I've never been until a professional work invitation means I am the sole face for my company.

At the end of the cul-de-sac, the first security guard greets me with an iPad in hand, escorting my eleven-year-old Sentra up the small driveway to the assigned valet, directing me then through a driveway full of lux-ury cars—two rows of four, all costing six figures at minimum—before another human with an iPad takes my and my partner's names, nodding to the man staring at us through the peephole at the middle-top of the main door.

I think the bass player of Metallica is in a full tuxedo. The lead singers of bands who have scored films, won Grammys, created music festivals mill about, sipping cocktails, a cool murmur of dialogue in the air but everyone talking in a polite hush. We know nobody and don't really care; I'm here to meet the host of the party, for whom the foundation is named, a skateboarder popular enough to have been previously sponsored by Bagel Bites and Hot Wheels. He's standing not too far away in new skate shoes and jeans, a nice shirt, his wife saying hi while their younger children, previously featured on their social media pages, hang out with presumed social media influencers just above their age demographic. A beautiful array of tables orbiting an outdoor fountain in the roofless garden awaits, the many wineglasses to be paired for each of the courses still being perfectly displayed by the staff. Security teams everywhere, telling you where to go, where's which bathroom, where you can proceed, and who can take pictures. Nearly everyone here is white, but nobody seems terribly snooty, given the circumstances. One of my favorite comedians is in a parakeet-bright V-neck a few folks away. A tall woman with a postured neck approaches us, asking us how we're doing, as if this sort of thing happens all the time. We do our best to maintain eye contact and smile before it becomes apparent we are as economically poor as the underwriting of this conversation, my drive here from the Bay Area riddled with fearful calculations about my recent oil change and whether I knew a guy in Bakersfield who could assist before the Grapevine potentially took me out.

The work contact who facilitated all of this for us suddenly arrives, equally shocked but in a suit and prepared, with a date, a young couple like us, given seat assignments for dinner. Sitting at our table are several board members, some presumed models, and that comic that I find hilarious. The famous musicians sit with the famous skater, standing now with the cook introducing the appetizer and the first batch of wine, of which only two barrels were made, specifically for this event, and a bottle will be auctioned off later for tens of thousands of dollars. But before that, the people at my table make introductions. The comedian makes eye contact with me and then looks away, whispering something to the board member next to him before he says, pointing at me, "I went to school with you."

"Seriously?"

"Yeah, I went to *school* with you," he notes, somewhat dramatically.

"You went to Berkeley?"

He nods. "I went to Berkeley."

"Man, that's crazy. I'm still up in the Bay Area."

"Oh. Berklee. Berklee School of Music."

We laugh, realizing the error, how close we came to being connected in some odd paradoxical way that leads to holding each other up for wine-barrel keg stands and embarrassing ourselves for a good cause and not getting thrown out of here, all that gone now because of a simple confusion of the two Berkeleys that anyone cares about.

Each course is amazing, the freshest, the best cooked; I hate wine and drink every paired glass. My partner is tuning out everything except the sound of her cutlery against the finished plate. The chef will soon be on the competitive cooking show *Top Chef*, around which memorabilia and viewer cooking-show nights are organized and produced and sold on repeat. I'm sure he hates everyone here and wants to smoke weed with the catering staff, with which he is more fraternal, but he is greatly and warmly appreciated.

Later, we watch a private performance by one of the guest musicians, whose band I saw on a punk lineup at the now defunct Irvine Meadows (and later Verizon Wireless Amphitheatre) and whose drummer broke a set of sticks on every song they played so hard (and well). The musicians, all millionaires, sit in respectful revenant awe during his solo performance, not a cell phone in sight documenting the performance, an unspoken rule of sorts emanating from this most private of cultures.

When we leave, they give us skateboard decks with the foundation's logo and the name of the cities where they've built parks worldwide. I notice the deck is signed by the extremely influential skateboarder in question and I briefly freak out, to the point that it isn't until I hit the highway that I realize I'd given the valet a twenty-dollar tip. Staying at a corporate-discounted hotel, we drive the 10 east toward the exit into downtown that goes right past the old Olympic Auditorium, and I point out to my girlfriend where, along West 18th Street, I stood with my friends for Rage Against the Machine's supposed last shows; my mother attended roller derby and dance nights there with her brothers throughout the 1960s and '70s; my cousins attended punk shows there during the venue's last years of its goings-on in the '80s and '90s. Until this night, the closest I've been to inside residential Beverly Hills was trying to find parking in high school for a show at the Troubadour.

Since the year 2000, California has weathered twelve of the fifteen largest fires in its history. The Mendocino Complex Fire, an amalgamation of the River and Ranch Fires, shot to the top of the list in 2018, with the Carr Fire at the sixth spot. Both transpired mere months after the Napa fires destroyed entire neighborhoods of Santa Rosa, with nearby Petaluma taking in hundreds of displaced families; the sky that week was a resin-black screen of smoke, clouds, and ash spreading sixty miles south across the Bay. Less than two weeks after the fundraiser dinner, the Skirball Fire engulfed the Bel Air neighborhood of Los Angeles, burning over four hundred acres of land along Sepulveda Boulevard and shutting down the University of California, Los Angeles, campus and those very parts of the 405 that I drove through to pick up my girlfriend at LAX. At one point during the 2018 summer, nineteen active fires burned statewide, including the historic Mendocino Complex and Carr Fires.

Two thousand California prisoners worked with Cal Fire to combat the flames threatening a landscape many would otherwise not see, not to mention risked their lives with the hope of being hired upon release. But none were employed upon completion of their sentences. Prisoners received a dollar an hour on top of a daily rate of two dollars for their labor. Firefighters average $74,000 a year in the state of California. Upon release, none of these inmates were eligible for hire because they weren't licensed EMTs. State licensing requirements enacted in dozens of counties require more than a year of education for the lowest on the pay scale; these licenses are required for a quarter of state jobs. Citing a recent Institute for Justice study, a *USA Today* article noted that "California ranked as the 'worst licensing environment for workers in lower-income occupations,' with the average license requiring a staggering 827 days of training. Absurdly, becoming a professional tree trimmer, barber, or painting contractor in California takes vastly more experience than becoming an EMT, who literally holds the lives of others in their hands."

We lived too inland for most of the larger wildfires growing up, but we weren't immune to earthquakes. Of those few memories shared across Los Angeles County, no incident takes greater precedent for my generation than the 1994 Northridge earthquake. Though the epicenter was over fifty miles west of our home in Pomona, everyone felt the violent force with which our world shook. Nine years old, I awoke to my father grabbing me, throwing me over his shoulder, and running down the short hallway dividing my and my sister's bedrooms, as I opened my eyes to the sight of my sister and mother following us, with sparks flying out of the thermostat mounted against the wall. We hid underneath a massive dining room table, supported by six thick legs and sturdy crossbeams, that is still in use today for hiding and eating alike. This was the trained emergency plan we learned in kindergarten, teachers preparing a generation of Southern Californians for all things tectonic disaster. Know your exits. Avoid gas ruptures and downed power lines. Find a door frame or bathtub. Avoid windows, threats of breaking glass. We stayed at a hotel down the street at the LA County fairgrounds for a day or two before power was restored.

A year before Northridge, I was introduced to natural disasters in third grade by the back of a T-shirt worn by one of the most popular kids. He was the best soccer player in school and heartthrob of the preps, and he came from a known local Mormon family. The nascent, perceived 1 percenters of this town were already aligned with the Church of Jesus Christ of Latter-day Saints or the types of Christian denominations that would evolve into megachurches by the time we graduated high school. But in 1992, after visiting one of his older siblings on a mission on the Big Island, he returned donning a T-shirt with I SURVIVED HURRICANE ANDREW emblazoned across his back in frenetic neon, like a disco was being torn apart by the hurricane and its shrapnel had landed in the design. An eight-year-old little brother wearing the shirt seemed more heroic than the mission to spread the word of Joseph Smith.

Yet I remember a year later, in 1994, thinking about whether every kid across Los Angeles County who felt something, who ran under a table, a door frame, whose parents grabbed them out of bed with all their might in those dramatic moments that define so much of our roles as parents, children, and the nebulous intersection in between, if we, too, would all get T-shirts at some point, and if they would look as dramatic as those given out on the acquired island of Hawai'i, designed for mainland dollars.

The ongoing joke about a California earthquake so strong that the state separates, finally, from the rest of the country was probably dreamed up in some midtown marketing agency as a latent fuck-you to the perception of the fun, sun, surf's-up lifestyle. Yet the front lawn of every newly sold home for newly arrived Californians already predicts our exterior-designed apocalypse, a waterless dry state, a cemetery of former agricultural empire.

The biggest question facing this state isn't just its survival but its destruction. A high-speed train barrels through the Central Valley, home to one of the world's key food supplies, a region that fears losing what little water it still has after years of forcing cash crops out of its soil and becoming a ghost town without water instead, and all I can remember when I think of our state dying are Bay Area conversations twenty years ago about how we'll never need air conditioning and, further back, a shard of a memory of me and my crew skating a loading dock in La Verne circa 1997, watching the red sun dye the Southern California sky a hue I'd never seen, basking in the sound of urethane wheels and a state I knew I'd never leave.

And now the question is whether it was real after all, whether our childhood setting wasn't just a virtual reality already up in smoke, as if California had already left the building, exited out the back door up the Los Angeles River, and hidden somewhere near Edwards Air Force Base—but then I remember those visceral, intrinsic moments when the earth beneath our skateboards shook, and we asked one another with our eyes, *Did you feel it?*, this California inquiry answered in our stares, an accepted knowledge that dreams exist in the same time and space as nightmares, that this land's last line of defense awakes in chains.

Daddy's Home

In his introduction to the world, Hirving "Chucky" Lozano receives the perfect pass across the 2018 Russian World Cup pitch from Javier "Chicharito" Hernández, creating a perfect opportunity for Chucky to stop and pivot the ball on a dime, spinning chest forward toward the goal, setting himself up for a well-squared Mexican cracker directly at the back of the defending world champion's German net. Instant legend status is immediately awarded to any twenty-two-year-old turning the world aflame with a single kick. Considering that my uncle didn't speak to anyone for a month after Argentina beat Mexico in 2006, this is good news for the Vadi household in Pomona, California. On Father's Day, no less. Fists clenched, our yells tinged with shock and joy, it is an amazing sight to behold on a Sunday morning when, like during so many sports events before, my dad is right next to me on the couch, not that we were the gender-normative stereotype of a Latin American version of *The Andy Griffith Show*, holding hands to the

fishing hole, but sports were our United Nations, where
political and social science collided.

The living room couch has changed since I moved
out in 2002, seemingly shrinking over time, and my
father is thankfully still there: A minor Hitchcockian
belly that has also, and even more thankfully, decreased
over time. His hair, a half 'fro of gray strands, nappy
and beautiful; a tank or a buttoned shirt and slacks; if
this were the later 1990s, a nearby heating pad and presumed empty mug; and during the '80s and '90s some
new issues of *LACMA*, *Foreign Policy*, *Current Affairs*, or
some other academic journal that he'd shit on but also
love and photocopy for his students, who, I'd learn while
holding his briefcase and sitting in on his first class post–
stomach surgery, were of a commuter-asshole breed who
could care less about anything political or science, and
I say this bitterly because I want to and can: I want students to know his pain of not having a TA for thirty-five
years and grading hundreds of blue books with actual
focus because he cared. School is always in session for
those educators who recognize the miseducation they
passed along their way, and they build a space-shuttle
launch of new knowledge every school year out of the
sliced district funding and out-of-pocket purchases that
schoolteachers like my mom made weekly. Or the constant reading, lecture-note preparing, publishing, and

grading of being a professor, all of that tension arriving home each night. We grew up on this silent, daily bell schedule alongside the fury of a professor tired of one-on-one meetings prompted by a blue book so badly written that he reaches out to the chancellor yet again for more support.

But I enjoyed the campus, his office near the quad, the mid-1990s internet that was a strong black cord inside his office, which was filled with books and art framed on the walls, a microcosmic example of our home. How the sky hung over the university, and Pomona Valley was so bright and oddly gorgeous on weekends when we had to go to the office for whatever silly reason. Maybe Pops was exercising some latent parental desire to see us watching the ol' man at the ol' plant, to correct, from his perspective, either our aloofness as children or our rebellion by the time of puberty—this skateboarding bullshit, this punk rock bullshit, what's he getting himself into, it's all wasted money not going toward tuition for schools he might not even get into—as all of life should lead to college and professions, the stereotypical immigrant dream that's increasingly weaponized the older I get. My parents focused on preparing us for the harsh reality that a grade compensated for whatever racist reactions the first name José generates in my professors', peers', and employers' eyes.

My parents nearly lost their minds supporting us. I have seen them flip out and drive away, tires screeching over parking blocks. If my fear of being a parent is the inability to live up to the standard mine created, their fears were the complete opposite. Forgiveness and a second, restored relationship with her parents found my mother's side of the family tree but not my father's. I feel like he was always maligned and not fully loved, and that we as a result tried to show twice, three times as much compassion to compensate for those negative forces, some of whom we never met, or only knew through crackled static Spanish calls to Florida and Aguada.

I have seen the abusive gaze of a grandfather I never met transfixed and transmitted through the furrowed, ruffled hatred of my father's eyes circa 1990-whenever-the-fuck, when I went to the master bedroom to see how he was doing after some momentary conflict. He looked up at me, right in the eye with an unforgettable sneer, asked, "What do you want?" on some tough-guy bullshit that I knew then and know now was barely a limp attempt at being the so-called patriarch his bloodline thought he should be. An ideal beaten into him by his own father. After years of therapy, medication, and travel for actual pleasure and not academic research, he has apologized and acknowledged that wrestling with his own demons led to him being insular during some key years there. He's said "You were right" about some of those rather odd decisions I made between my early twenties and now, and it's hard to accept the knowledge that nothing gets swept under the rug in a home of historians, a shit metaphor considering most rugs are thin as hell.

Chucky's goal sets the living room, the house, the city, the county, the globe into collective relief and simultaneous frenzy, briefly calming my dad's nerves physicalized during any game through tics and screams, like a teenager watching their heartthrob comb their hair on Ed Sullivan. The childhood of my father's Harlem transmitted itself again through his demeanor— the gregariousness of the dudes on the corner of La Marqueta in East Harlem circa 1951; the bullshit dozens emitted from throats my father wanted to wring because they stole from the family bodega; the fists he threw against Italian gangs' cheeks on the wrong side of 3rd Avenue before he raised them on the steps of the civil rights movement in Madison, Wisconsin. When I was growing up, my father always seemed in a fog, caught between worlds, with an immeasurable ability to float above any sense of reality and immerse himself back into being that boy in a corner of a tenement full of Puerto Ricans migrating their way into Nueva Yor'. A world where he and his older brother were routinely punished, my grandfather's cruelty on full tilt, a man I never met, whose tomb may or may not still exist in Aguada with my uncle and grandmother after the most recent hurricanes and lack of U.S government relief. Whose face is embalmed on the walls of our parents' homes in California.

A man I want to punch squarely in the face, whose name I did not take in vain when I met my grandmother, his wife, in Aguada for the first time when I was fifteen. I remember his name, Heladio, and that's all I need to know about the bastard who stripped my dad of the ability to know his true self, forced him to need acceptance to fill the void Heladio created with grades and academia, the empirical truth found in academic prowess, the only sanity amid the inherent stress of academic-dependent Presidents' Scholarships. He was a kid from Benjamin Franklin High School, East Harlem, alma mater of Joe Bataan, having shown up in America's heartland on a hunch with barely a suitcase to his name upon arrival; he had Manhattan childhood memories of running in the Millrose Games at Madison Square Garden, of being a neighborhood face with the likes of Jimmy Baldwin and sharing some of the same mentors at CCNY. I wonder if Baldwin was at the same sermon at Mosque No. 7 where my father witnessed Malcolm X leading and preaching before his first audiences, in pursuit of that guidance and control he never had on 116th and Park.

Father's Day morning swiftly continues with the commute that starts in the middle of the street: my mother, when anxious, just starts driving, parking the minivan directly on the yellow line of a street that, when approached from the uphill cross street, puts us directly in the blind spot of oncoming traffic. There are no apologies for this act, just an additional request to turn around and make sure the door's locked. She is a self-defined LA girl who reveres her collection of Doors and Joni Mitchell records just as much as her Brenda and the Tabulations 45s, whose short, spiky, salt-and-pepper hair I've known my whole life, who once donned wigs down past her shoulders while attending Mt. San Antonio College in the late 1960s with many of her classmates from Bassett High School, the relatively new school that combined all the sets of Bassett within La Puente, those on the side of Valley Boulevard closest to the 60 freeway, no longer bused to nearby Arroyo or El Monte High but all now here, fighting for their own turf in the halls and locker room showers.

It is at this school that my mother's derriere touched linoleum when she was pushed by a *chola* whose crew stood on the sidelines waiting to intervene, and *cholas* are cool, as are *cholos*—it's not about gangsters, just descriptions—and their description of my mother was *güera, gabacha,* equivalents of Uncle Tom for Chicanas when they were assumed to be passing instead of having actual immigrant roots, as my mother did, a product of laborers and farmworkers and Brown Okies and living off nopales and reeds sucked dry for nutrients when times were frequently rough. Those moments became a montage of jump cuts before my mother's furious eyes, as she got off the linoleum and turned that other girl's face a shade of purple that said, "Like I said, leave me alone." Which is exactly what the leader of the opposing pack said when her crew wanted to jump in for revenge; the numbers were on their side, but the crew was otherwise not involved in the pushing *chola*'s beef, their leader J saying, "She asked for it, she got it," and that was that. Some of those same *cholas* would later do my mother's hair and makeup on her wedding day nearly ten years later in a La Puente backyard in 1975, but even by senior year their leader J and her sister would be the ones my mom hung out with for a Southern California tradition: the Disneyland grad-night all-nighter.

After a 7:00 p.m. graduation ceremony, high school seniors are bused from all across Los Angeles and Orange Counties, the San Gabriel Valley and Inland

Empire, for an all-night party at Disneyland, a student-and-chaperone takeover of the theme park until dawn. Somehow my grandfather said yes and paid for the ticket, a little over ten dollars in 1968 (her five older brothers pooled together additional pocket cash), and off she went with two girlfriends, all introduced via a freshman-year fight, all three now with diplomas and damn near falling asleep on the Magic Kingdom's benches.

Standing behind the minivan, I ask my mom why she parked in the middle of the street, me the youngest and somehow the only inquisitive member of my family in these moments, and she replies, "I don't know." I'm still not sure how to identify her anxious ghosts, the expectation specters haunting her moves still two years into retirement, but what do I know? I turn around at her request to make sure the door's locked, and we drive to the other side of the 405 from the far side of "where the 10, 210, and 57 meet"—Los Angeles County's farthest eastern corridor, the mouth of the San Gabriel Valley, the first breaths of the Inland Empire.

The minivan replaced the Oldsmobile and the Buick LeSabre (nicknamed "the Buck" because of a missing *i* on the front dashboard) when I went to college, for some reason. Maybe it was because my mom knew I was moving back to Los Angeles after Berkeley, and she was ready to cargo me home at my temporary Northern Californian disposal. Either way, the 60, aka the Pomona Freeway, is moving steadily as we pass the familiar Whittier Boulevard exit, where my mom hums the opening holler from the title track of Thee Midniters' infamous song, and my dad comments on how homelessness, particularly where the freeways meet the Los Angeles River and the relatively new 710 freeway, has persisted since before my sister and I were born. No Olympics bid or downtown rejuvenation project could impact homelessness without first addressing its socioeconomic and contributing causes; how many conversations happen like this in cars heading to the Getty, talking this type of shit so early after a Mexico victory? I reply to myself, "More than you realize, stupid." Except even I don't have the types or numbers of examples to say that fact for sure. But I do daydream about the Nancy Garcias and David Gonzalezes of my high school honors classes, the only other Latin-identifiable kids, and pray that, unlike other members of my extended bloodline, they don't forget where they come from at the ballot box.

High enough on the 405 now that the Getty exit isn't blocked by traffic, we arrive early for the free tram snaking along the hills of folks coming from Valencia down I-5 and through the remnants of the Skirball Fire that nearly scorched this entire center down. A lifetime of work was put into this massive, free, and somewhat-accessible-by-car (i.e., walking in Los Angeles) museum with its pulley-system tram that runs through shrubbery toward the top of the hill for a southward view of the city and the Pacific Ocean. Before 1997, the DIY version of this was going up and down the Century Building tower's elevator, safely getting a view of the whole city for free.

My stomach starts doing backflips when I exit the tram—not the tram's fault, it's just an underlying feeling now reaching the wrong type of height at an even worse moment, maybe digesting the guilt of living on the other side of the state, of not being a lawyer (however forgiven by my mother), of not staying true to Los Angeles even though I grew up in its badlands, and of the desire to live up to the concept of the Good Son to a father who had *the* worst familial experience. Maybe my intestinal lining, too, was shook, my eyes darting around the myriad buildings and wings of the Getty for restrooms and drinking fountains, everything swirling in that hazy, early-morning west-side heat, my family staring at a map, each alpha politely telling the other what to do. In this case, my father has the privilege of leading, meaning my mother will take his desired goals and play the role of quarterback, with my sister the glue between, while I leverage both my stomach and my traditional role as exhibit scout to go a few rooms ahead of everyone, mentally mapping which rooms had the era, form, and style of paintings that my dad and the others want to see.

Today: modernism, oils, not the touristy shit. I realize C has probably been here enough times to tell me where to go, so I quickly send him a chat on my phone— "Take me to the modernist shit (plz, @ getty, big one)"— amid this outdoor tribute to a man so wealthy and cheap that, as my father noted upon seeing Getty's bust near the entry doors, "all of this, and even after getting his grandson's ear in the mail, he *still* negotiated the ransom." And Dad's right, I realize, walking toward the farthest pavilions. The realization that this is *my* first time here hits me; when I previously visited in 2001, the center wasn't nearly as complete as it is today. Or maybe that was the Getty Villa. Probably. Los Angeles is known and unknown, memory and mystery alike, and I have been away as many years as those raised in this county's eastern cut.

C replies immediately, "West Building - 2nd floor: James Ensor's Christ's Arrival at Brussels," and I scurry past the Monets and Van Goghs and the tours of headphone-adorned humans standing in half circles, blocking any and all paths, and I find the room at the farthest end of the building, with a massive wall-sized mural that is amazingly vibrant and ridiculously farcical in its detail: two men shitting and vomiting on the acronyms of their former political parties scrawled across a balcony overlooking Christ's parade into town, everyone taking the moment to turn Jesus's arrival into whatever spectacle they want the moment to represent, which may be religion itself, or politics, I can't say for sure. The usher politely informs me, "No photos of any kind for this one," and I turn around and find my parents intrinsically on time to the cadence genetically and socially constructed between the four of us since my arrival in 1984. They, too, share the awe that I have, that C showed me (he's there, cousin in spirit via phone), and it's almost overwhelming, walking around each corridor of the Getty, up and down the stairs, with my parents, in their sixties and seventies, imagining them doing the same when they toured Spain recently together, both now retired; how I worry about them, and how infrequently the four of us exist as a unit, together again, and then it swirls in my mind that I am about to faint, I need to find the washroom again to expel, like in the mural, the vomit and fear and pain down any drain that I can find, the pipelines descending from north of Sac down south.

After my body beats itself up for whatever cause, I reunite with my family in front of the restaurant for our reservation, more dazed than confused, before I feel my father's arm rise toward mine, making a falling shawl for my shoulder blades, when he says, "I miss you, Son," and it all hits me. It could be the bile still on my breath or the way the sun moving across this patio hits most of my skin, but the desire to pass out returns in the form of sunglasses-covered tears hidden long enough to make the entry into the restaurant's lobby as smooth as possible on a holiday when everyone looks like a peacock or the aloof, entitled, fresh signature of an eviction notice in church shoes.

I don't know whether to think our waiter's racist or at the very least biased when, after my mother begins asking about changing her fixed-price-menu beer selection for something nonalcoholic, he cuts her off and replies, "Whatever it is or not, it probably won't cost any more than the fixed price you see here," when no inquiry regarding cost was made. I expected something like that to happen before we sat down, but thankfully decorum is restored and my mother's long stare back at the waiter denotes that she, unlike many, doesn't want alcohol at noon, and he removes his foot from his mouth long enough to take our orders. I order a French toast situation that will hopefully mend but knowingly aggravate the walls of my stomach, but nothing else looks appeasing on a menu built for Instagram algorithms, and I'll probably vomit anyway. My parents continue to

stave off the guilt of the fixed price, a routine price for
so many company lunches and Bay Area get-togethers
that are even more Hollywood than their Silicon Beach
peers, and the toast helps the stomach after all, my body
feeling more human as we descend post-meal into the
massive garden rolling down the Astroturfed hills,
where children tumble and dates awkwardly interrogate
each other on the timely matter of dad issues, I assume,
and I wait for the perfect opportunity to document my
family actually *enjoying* being together as a foursome
for maybe the last time ever. Who knows, I could get
sucked out of my Southwest flight on the way home, I
think, and we find the base of the garden shaped like
a mini-labyrinth, with Greco-Roman columns and
wheelchair accessibility (unlike the Colosseum), and I
ask a beautiful older couple in matching white workout
outfits if they can take a photo of the four of us after
they're done doing matching Wakanda poses, and the
woman responds, "Do you have an hour?" before the
man art-directs us for what feels like five minutes but is
really thirty seconds longer than the five usually allotted
to such citizen teamwork.

Families are papier-mâché levels of balance, emo-
tionally, socially, and historically, and each moment
shared is a time-stamped reminder of what's occurred
and what can never be again. For a family that can make

itself feel guilty about any decision, morale in my family is high. Expectations are met. Arguments mitigated and cut off at the pass. There is no wallowing in previous victimizations, however justified and necessary the grievances; negativity is not consuming my father, nor stress my mother and sister, and whatever disconnected jadedness I can project as still, and forever, the youngest isn't affecting me either. And when my mom asks if I want to drive, I of course say yes, willing and able to lead this minivan through weekend 405 south traffic, directly into the eye of the storm that is LAX, and get my sister to her flight on time and safely so she can arrive in our state's capital for her rotation the next morning, saving children one operation at a time. Oh, how beautiful we are before I hear my sister yell, "Too close!" just as this boat of a minivan makes a right turn and clips the corner of a parked Mercedes-Benz. I stop the car; the weight in my stomach becomes a pit I imagine being twisted by three pairs of hands bearing my same bloodline, and double-parked now, my mother stands by the empty Benz, taking photos and jotting down license plate numbers and trying to get reception in the submerged third-floor parking garage beneath a rich man's trust.

The catastrophic thinking about myself that Kaiser Permanente's psychiatry and behavioral health department taught me in 2008 begins to unravel again a decade later; all the 45s I played the night before from my mother's collection, Brenda and the Tabulations, War, El Chicano, mean nothing now, those previous joys consumed by my current failure. And how earnest it was, that sonic attempt to drown out the noise from the house a few streets down, where former IBF lightweight champion of the world and Pomona native "Sugar" Shane Mosley was hosting a rager of a Father's Day party—ironic for a boxer who fired his own father as his manager before they reunited two years later. As kids, we'd run into Mosley at Ganesha Park during his rise circa 1997–98, the champ telling us we were crazy for jumping on the concrete benches by the basketball half-courts with our skateboards when he was getting in the ring with a dude who's twice his height for his next HBO fight. I recalled how blue his eyes were back then, and how coolly he jogged up and down the park, and how much I wanted to be like him, and now look at me, in the bottom of some godforsaken privately owned parking facility, my mother freaking out, my sister silent (received initially as smugness, when really it's the zen of a medical professional who categorically sees much worse on a daily basis), and my father also silent and just feeling very, very bad for me, his son, as he always does, because he, like my mother, wants the best for me—what

everyone wants for one another and the underlying reason we're all in the van to begin with. They assure me
that "it's an honest mistake," "it's why I have insurance,"
it's this and that, and all I can see is my knees and the cat
hair carried over from my Oakland apartment on the
flight thirty thousand feet above the fields my grandfather tilled in Gonzales and how it's all folly now. My
sister will surely be late and miss her flight, and I'll return the rental car late to Ontario Airport (and forget to
gas up where Inland Empire Boulevard hits Archibald
beforehand), and everything's going to be fucked because of this one fuckup, and it's then that I put my sunglasses back on, holding back a river now, and my mom
automatically opens the sliding door with her key fob,
grabs me by the shoulders, and says, "Hey. Hey. It's not
your fault. It's not your fault."

LAX is trash—not surprising. We grin and bear it
and discuss how a cousin's landscaping firm helped in-
stall those massive vertical column lights around the
entrance, how every televised Lakers or Clippers game
cuts away to them. My sister gives me a nice long smile
before she says goodbye to everyone, making nice to my
parents upon dismount, big hugs and notifications ensured upon arrival, she promises. Every time I say goodbye to my sister, I think of being an undergraduate at
Cal and taking BART to MUNI, as she taught me to do

back when I was a junior high kid visiting *her* at Cal,
but this time I'm heading all the way out to 17th Avenue
during her stint at UCSF Medical School. Sometimes
we'd meet downtown for dinner, and afterward at the
Civic Center BART, in the space between BART's and
MUNI's entrances, I'd wait and watch her descend the
escalator to her outbound N Judah train, as I'd take the
Richmond back home. She'd always face me and wave,
smiling. The older I get, the more I realize how much
of the gnarly era of San Francisco she encountered as a
resident in San Francisco General's psych ward, hearing the tales of patients obsessed with Metallica to the
degree that they *know* they're in the band and need to
get out of the facility to go on tour. Our caravan of three
now immediately reminds me of high school, when it
was just my parents and me, with me running amok in
the streets, skateboarding after honors classes and choir
all day, thinking about my sister at Stern Hall, how good
the pizza slices (slices!) and record stores were on Telegraph Avenue, and how I'd rather be on BART than in
a car any day of a Southern California week. Silly now,
but it's when I say goodbye to her, realizing how similar
we look, that I realize that I've been following her path
all along. Until now. Plaza Mexico sign off the 105 before
the 605, and I have to take a selfie, sending it to C at
home in nearby Paramount. I wonder what he'll notice

more, the sign or the red in my eyes, but probably neither, shouting out the sign's location more than anything
else. *Location's everything*, says the opportunistic realtor,
but those from here know it shapes an entire choose-
your-own-adventure story that never changes over time,
just becomes more complicated.

By the time my mom shook sense into my cry-
ing self in the parking lot, she'd already filed a claim
with the insurance company. She lies down when we
get back home, my dad watering the St. Augustine in
the backyard that has stayed miraculously green despite water regulations, proud of his self-trained green
thumb. I walk up the hill to this little streetlamp under
which I used to write my first poems on some unknow-
ingly Joe Bataan shit, and walk higher still to a view
of the county fairgrounds. I walk a few blocks more
toward the other side of the hill, finding the first curb I
ollied up, and an open house: a new home on what was
once a private plot of dirt that was the perfect neighborhood vantage point for the LA County fairgrounds'
annual July 4 fireworks show entitled KABOOM!, a
small consolation for bearing the sonic brunt of explo-
sions all night, everyone from all over driving in for
the annual celebration of a colorful sky and a vague
palpable sense of patriotism. That piece of dirt is now a
three-story hillside home with a view, listed at just over

eight hundred thousand dollars. When I enter the open house, I take off my hat, smooth my hair, and replace my black shades with prescription specs. Two women greet me, pamphlets in hand, offering the moon and more, thankfully allowing me to take a peek solo. Massive bedrooms, tons of space, an expectation of family or roommates . . . so odd to consider this all in a community where people came to live and retire, where I, my sister, and my neighbor's Catholic-schoolgirl-but-punk daughters were the only young folks on the block.

My parents are concerned more about the asking price when I come home. Mom and I chat at the kitchen table as my dad practices jazz guitar in the other room, having learned to read sheet music in his seventies, successfully. We naturally get to talking about oldies, the songs I played the night before from her collection, the infamous *Art Laboe Connection*—something both of us grew up with and never knew a life without—and I ask her if she's ever heard the frequent caller Emma request The Manhattans, and she sees my references and raises me her memory of a caller from East LA who would always dedicate "Daddy's Home" by Shep and the Limelites to her husband who died in Vietnam, my mom thinks, and when she died, the kids picked up the phone, every night, calling in the track for both their parents now, a tradition. That seemingly could only happen in Los

Angeles, yet we both now listen to Art Laboe through web browsers on our phones, as listeners dial in from Nevada, Arizona, New Mexico.

I show my mom the mobile anamorphic lens and iPhone Shure mic I've been using for some of my reporting and amateur film projects, and per her suggestion (and my implication) I test the new lens by shooting my father in the other room, maneuvering its interface by walking quietly, softly, from the entryway into the dining room, shooting the vinyl collection and massive murals and paintings we grew up staring at and that created the implicit sense of creativity and wonder that has always visually and sonically filled this home since 1986, panning slowly to my father sitting between a rack of string instruments—guitars, *laúdes*, *cuatros*—and my sister's piano, a gallery of framed family photos lining its lid: deceased cousins, graduation photos, recent internet-downloaded and printed photos, new grandchildren from outer reaches of the family tree, all there in the background of this wide-angle shot. It takes everything for me not to nod along, not to shake the shot, as my dad slowly plays George Harrison's "My Sweet Lord," knowing this is a rough draft of something he'll play intuitively by the end of the summer.

It's in these moments that I don't want to leave on time down the 10 east to make my flight at a presumably deserted Sunday night Ontario International Airport; it's on these nights that I want to come back to something I left nearly two decades prior, a Los Angeles I now know absolutely nothing about but periodically engage with and stay abreast of through friends and relatives and local news but really through imagination and memory and the gray areas in between. Yet how did I know those cranes just east of the 405 were a forthcoming stadium? How do I never look at maps here and still get there, always? "Intrinsic" is the word but "possessed" is the feeling: I will never understand Los Angeles and never want to—it's not the point.

The newly revamped airport NASCAR-themed bar is open and still not intriguing. A Brown man gives me a head nod in the hallway and later sits next to me on the "very full flight" to Oakland. I move to the middle seat to allow an older gentleman the presumed physical benefit of the aisle, however threatening those snack carts are to his elbows. I usually do the opposite, pay extra fees for more room and more seating time, all in the name of preventing anxiety, of establishing a sense of control before going thirty thousand feet above the ground; I always imagine what we're flying over, and over the years have gotten to know that map better and better, even the Sierras. The guy offers me some Whoppers that he pulls from his bag, telling me he got them

from his daughter, that she got him a whole box knowing they're his favorites. I wonder whether she's going
to request a call for him on *The Art Laboe Connection*,
whether he's heading north to start a weeklong truck
route or if something else, for whichever of life's many
reasons, leads him to this seat on this flight and his
daughter to the snack aisle. "They're delicious," I say.
"Thank you."

Upon arrival in Oakland, I wait for a yellow cab while
two North Beach, San Francisco, residents ask for a yellow cab at the taxi kiosk, then negotiate on their phones
for better prices, then ask again for the cab that is still on
its way here. On 880, the Warriors stare back at me, stoic
in their back-to-back-champion grace, and I whisper to
myself, "One more year," knowing they'll be in the city
by 2020, wondering how loud the new "Roaracle" will be
(if ever). I text my family in Los Angeles, letting them
know I'm back in Oakland, as the cabbie curves around
Laney College, around the downtown skyline and the
Tribune Tower, its red font an unparalleled glow, lower
than the buildings and cranes around it. How many
times have I been in car-related incidents in this damn
state, and how long will I sleep here before I am saying
goodbye again to an Oakland four hundred miles north
of an inland childhood—navigable, distressing, chaotic,
familiar—and will my mother accept my offer to cover

the damages for the van, and will my father allow himself to enjoy another Father's Day like this again, and will I allow myself to do the same, whether or not I'm behind any wheel?

Spot Check

Crack cocaine is a part of the design of every good skate park in the world, and I miss its San Francisco source. Upon its 1980s introduction to San Francisco, crack was colloquialized to simply "hubba," and in the vernacular of early 1990s skate culture, it became immortalized in the tree-ensconced and just-out-of-reach-of-the-main-pedestrian-path spot called Hubba Hideout, a derelict quasi lair and skate spot, where there's a pedestrian bridge with two concrete ledges that serve as both walls and handrails, at the end of which six stairs drop into a small plaza of red bricks surrounded by eucalyptus and redwood trees, a small sitting area for Financial District coffee breaks and tai chi practice. More than thirty years after Wade Speyer christened the spot with a backside nosegrind, Hubba Hideout became so famous and recognizable that any massive concrete ledge going down a set of stairs is referred to as a hubba, in the popular, soon-to-be-Olympic vernacular.

I remember taking photos of Hubba Hideout when I

was thirteen and visiting from Southern California, my dad lurking behind me but encouraging me to shoot the vacant brick staircase, which now had metallic knobs on its worn ledges, recently attached to prevent future sessions, memories, achievements, and paychecks. The memory of that first roll of black-and-white is one in a lifetime of reasons I take an early Transbay bus across the Bay Bridge into the city before work and walk through some of the oldest and newest buildings south of Market near the Fremont Street off-ramp. The green marble sea of the Sailors' Union of the Pacific building's steps flows into a small cocoon of concrete bordered by an end wall, and the busy streets of Harrison and 1st on either side create the perfect subterfuge of a spot. No hubbas here, just the smooth marble ground and a massive set of stairs. The thick prohibitive chain at the top of the stairs is gone, so you know there have been sessions.

When I roll across the pavement today, however infrequently, I still hear the songs from the videos that introduced me to the very lines, pathways, and setups I subconsciously navigated through schoolyards and ditches, manual pads, and staircases. But it's visiting historic spots as a so-called skate tourist or as an actual skater that feels like an accomplishment just by being there, an homage to the possibility skateboarding always offers if you're willing to try and destroy yourself in the process. I know that the first crosstown 38-Geary bus leaves Montgomery off Market just before 7:00 a.m., taking me all the way to Sutro Baths and nearby Fort Miley, whose barracks are one of the most famous skate obstacles still sessionable in the whole city. I know this city's landmarks as a skateboarder and an educator, a college student, a professional. Yet no matter how many degrees I earn or jobs I work in this city, and no matter how many gold medals skateboarding will engender on behalf of the United States beginning in the 2020 Olympic Games, street skateboarding will always be a crime, permitted only so long as the spot is out of pedestrian sight. At Embarcadero, the small wheel-and-axle marks of the day are imprinted at the bottom of the surrounding three-stair that divides plaza from eating area and on top of which the misfits who defined this city's style once talked shit, ditched school, escaped broken homes, and created their own world. Spots like this still feel like an actual, concrete family photo album that's been fractured, scattered, and frequently altered but still together and surviving, these former and familiar imprints of themselves, me and my body searching all the same.

I go that morning to take a photo of the ledge that pro skater turned actor Jason Lee backside tailslid near one of two large statues, but then I meet, or rather encounter,

Dale—white dude, ponytail, groundsman—who's definitely noticed me taking pictures.

"You like the building?"

"I love the architecture," I say, not mentioning that it's skateable or that I'm fantasizing about sailing over and down the marble steps with a massive switch heelflip, like the departed Keenan Milton, in a clip from the Spike Jonze–directed skate videos I immediately illegally downloaded via Kazaa upon arrival to a UC Berkeley dormitory, using the broadband internet I had limited access to in high school. Dale doesn't need to know that, with his morning coffee thermos in hand and bearing the resemblance of a longshoreman turned farmer turned city skipper.

"C'mon man! I'll show you the whole building!"

His hand goes to the holster full of keys that remind me of some old coworker's comment about my keys circa 2007 and how they'd hang off a clip—I'd never want to have so many keys, like I'm a janitor, but Dale's keys open the door to a massive main lobby, a sort of waiting room, a maritime labor terminal.

"In a few hours this place will be filled with sixty, eighty folks looking for work around the world."

Dale shows me this all-white male auction block painting depicting some interpretation of a historic scene circa 1901 or something, praising the yesteryear depicted in-frame, and it's all mighty polite of him to paint a praiseworthy portrait for me, talking about how the theater upstairs is still functioning, just not publicly accessible, same with the bar and the barbershop downstairs, all private rentals now.

We head back outside to stare at the building, taking in the historical all, and he starts a type of sermon I've heard since I started skateboarding in 1996, something about "Yeah man, these skateboarders" this and that, scratching off marble that has outlasted enough earthquakes to decimate a warehouse of skateboards in a single blow, marble that is more damaged by the amoeba-like shell skate stoppers, those preventative, defensive objects knobbed to the pedestrian spaces and benches at every new development in the city. He says something about how the dude who designed these stoppers is so in demand that there's a waiting list for his coveted aquatic designs, a craftsman focused on the art of his work indeed, and about how he was the same dude who did one of the larger antiskate retrofits the city's ever seen, destroying the concrete ledges that once divided the Embarcadero's pedestrian path. Per the script—"Don't get me wrong, I used to skate, but I got older and times changed, man"—he stretches those last notes into an empathic tone, and I agree, because he is right and not wrong, it's fucking vandalism, yes, but isn't

it odd that this spot is history to some jackass like me
and thousands of others who can glance at something
from (gasp) twenty years ago, something that qualifies
as a state landmark but that we, too, see as historical?
That we, too, view as landmarkable, something to bear
witness to and appreciate?

He discusses the two statues outside, two heads of
men who apparently helped create the very maritime
unions utilized today. I loosely mention tariffs, the kind
dominating the headlines recently between China and
the United States, within hours of our chance encounter, and I ask him whether he's seen any impact here in
the building, given his front-row seat to supply and demand personified. He says, "Too early to tell, everyone's
still waiting to see," before identifying himself as a cen-
trist who leans Democrat; he didn't vote for Hillary but
didn't vote for the president as of writing. He goes further, mentioning something about how "we don't even
know what the president and Russia are necessarily lying
about," and it's that inflated sense of truth that speaks to
a conspiracy-leaning news source I imagine is popular
wherever he leaves from to head into the city. Political
conversations aside, the fact (for me at least) remains
that we are at a historic skate spot, a lens into a world of
intersections of repetitive physicalized forms turned artistic borderline-sports practice. And like most skaters

unrecognized at a spot, I try to dip before he is somehow able to notice that, from my shoes to my hat, there are skater influences and brands that relate to the marble ground of this historic, beautifully preserved building and even more so to its scratches, its impact marks, its prohibitive chains, and ugly skate stoppers. This is my subtle connection to an explicitly loud act, wearing the trademark skater-with-a-job shoe, an all-black skate shoe, and somehow this guy gives me the pass inside to the halls where another, older gig economy begins. "I like that you don't want to talk politics," he says. "It's too early anyway." And I agree, shaking his hand, saying "thanks for the tour" and "goodbye," walking down Harrison toward work on the other side of SoMa.

Labor and physical space. Day laborers vulnerable on the side of the street versus the organized and unionized presumed "order" of the maritime building's daily trade. I remember passing the LinkedIn headquarters on Fremont before Harrison, its lobby advertised as one of dozens of Privately Owned Publicly Open Spaces popular in the nouveau-tech era of San Francisco's arguable third tech boom. Its massive wood-panel walls balance gleaming white floors, multiple chairs, and sofas and benches, open to all who presumably aren't homeless or otherwise in need. An accessible space, a lobby without questions, which was damn near the presumption with most spaces in the city, not necessarily a selling point. Compare that to the welcome mat I received from Dale.

And what to make of this white truck turned van I encounter on my walk to work in an alley just off Harrison, before 6th Street dips beneath the freeway overpass and near the Coca-Cola sign, these alleys full of parked cars and parked tents, those without homes finding shelter with what nearby amenities and shelter an overpass provides? Connected to the back of a van with bungee cords is a Department of Public Works gate that would otherwise block homeless folks from propping tents on the sidewalks (a trademark tactic of Mayor Lee's administration now carried over by Mayor London Breed), and there's a well-scrawled sign that reads PATENT ATTORNEY and a 415 phone number. On the alley's corner at Harrison is a mechanic's shop that years ago was dedicated to repairing Caterpillar agricultural and industrial equipment. The side of the building still bears a mural by Don Clever commemorating this era of western industrial prowess, the so-called Caterpillar Mural, where men with massive biceps trudge rocks with Caterpillar tools up and down the gold rush mountains that seem so foreign here in a land of Dolores Park picnic blankets. The mural is noted by local preservationists and nominated to be registered as a California state landmark, covered by an awning and surrounded by a spiked fence, creating the metropolitan equivalent of a moat around its rich painted surface. One of my favorite skateboarders and former San Francisco resident Brian Anderson recently ollied over the fence (and maybe the sidewalk) in an editorial photo for *Thrasher* magazine, a massive ollie over a spiked black fence into an alleyway whose gutters are filled with coping mechanisms and discarded decisions. That photo got Anderson paid while the handwritten sign remains, waiting for opportunity and profit to wishing-well itself into existence. Maybe the sign is instead a beeping signal of life, a visualized self-recognition of those attempts to survive amid the changing waves of labor, space, and time that is San Francisco.

My relationship with the city is sometimes a willful dice roll: I hear about a skate spot with some modicum of local history that's still around, and off I go into the far reaches of MUNI, planning an afternoon or early morning jaunt around the destination and finding tomfoolery, the beauty of living in a city for a lifetime and still being able to explore with a skater's unique, original, and destructively perceptive eye. A Godzilla movie marathon at one of the art deco theaters in the Avenues I had never visited seems like the perfect excuse to explore spots on San Francisco's west side.

The WELCOME TO PRESIDIO sign has a tacked-on placard warning of the active presence of mountain lions throughout the area at all times of day, especially at night. I look up toward the sunset and the Golden Gate Bridge's intimidating pillars in the distance, noticing how the most recent wildfire smoke evaporates into a singed fog across the northernmost point of San Francisco. Maybe the tourists smartly walking in the opposite direction read me as some urban-adventure-trail type, going head-on into the elements, when really I'm just a stupid pedestrian turned civilian lurker, searching for a concrete retention wall that, shaped like a wave or launch ramp, turned into a spot in the mid 1990s documented with a fish-eye lens and looking like a back-alley Camelot, a random apartment building surrounded by tall skinny trees.

I had already taken BART from Oakland to the Sunset via the N Judah to look at one spot, the massive set of stairs at Abraham Lincoln High School that Jim Greco, Andrew Reynolds, and Jerry Hsu have immortalized, before walking along the Sunset Reservoir on 24th Avenue through the Sunset and into Golden Gate Park, indulging in a tourist snack-cart thirst trap of a pretzel and root beer at Spreckels Lake, observing the miniboat schooner racers at the northeast corner, remembering when my dad was here a few years back. I took him out to Beach Chalet, the restaurant overlooking the Pacific and the PCH and walking back with him through most of Golden Gate Park to the de Young. How rare that simple thing was and still is, as I sit here now and take a break, as my ankles have trouble bending properly, doing this cocked half step that reminds me of the charred surviving remains of Fire Marshall Bill of *In Living Color*–era Jim Carrey fame, swollen from commuter-turned-superlurker use, and I'm not even at the Richmond yet.

Opened in 1926, the Balboa Theater on 38th Avenue and Balboa is an art deco nickelodeon theater converted into a two-screen preservationist dreamboat in the 1970s, the remodels done by the same folks behind Cliff House and several other theaters, preserving a part of the Outer Richmond that kisses the Pacific. In an era of exclusive movie runs of *The Sound of Music* and *Doctor Zhivago* at theaters on Market Street, this neighborhood gem introduced the Outer Lands to equally long runs of *The Sound of Music* in a neighborhood of a handful of locals-only holes-in-the-wall stretching six avenue blocks.

The Godzilla festival is a mini-Comic-Con of sorts, centered around a singular personification of Japanese dread, fear, anger, and paranoia in the wake of a devastating Second World War and repeated nuclear bombings.

144 /INTER STATE

The rare, imported Japanese toys and life-sized Mothra doll are less enthralling than the architecture and availability of beer from the corduroy art students behind concessions. Twenty minutes into the first of three movies I remember that the movie in question, *Godzilla vs. Mothra*, is indeed the worst Godzilla movie of all time, nowhere close to its 1960s counterparts in terms of generating sheer fear and reflecting, however absurdly, the extremely real effects of 1945. Thankfully the dozen or so milligrams of medicinal marijuana in a chocolate espresso bean I'd taken kick in just as the movie ends, fueling my flight out of the theater and to a nearby coffee shop that seems more like a community space than a for-profit caffeine dispensary: dozens of roasts and brew methods on-site, locals writing and reading, kids on skateboards stopping in to get food after bombing Balboa. Their boards are sparkling in quality, even the scratches almost perfectly executed across the bottoms.

Destruction is intrinsic to skateboarding: fear, gender barriers, shoelaces, board graphics, aluminum, marble, concrete, urethane all must perish for skateboarding to exist. Skateboarding poses an inherent challenge to the working-class ideal of buying something that'll last as long as economically and functionally possible; it trains you to buy products designed to be destroyed as a necessary means to a product's end. My dad would use wood putty on the tail of my worn board before re-drilling the wheelbase—"ghetto ingenuity," my father called it—trying to keep the deck going for as long as possible because, for whatever economically rational reason, my parents didn't want to buy a twenty-eight-dollar new blank plus five dollars for grip tape every month from the shop just for me to fall on my ass all over the driveway and destroy sprinkler heads left and right. My parents were exasperated by my extracurricular bullshit, my pubescent frame full of arms and energy trying to jump off everything in sight.

The kids at the coffee shop remind me of spots at nearby schools, Presidio Middle School and George Washington High School, and how the latter has New Deal–commissioned murals inside the lobby and maybe a skate spot or two, and my mind continues to wander and remember that nearby is Richmond Playground, showcased in the seminal skate-movie classic *The Search for Animal Chin*, which burned images of the original Bones Brigade into my mind, as they lugged and propped a jump ramp against a handball wall for a wallride session and cinematic history. I feel the fog turn into a calm drizzle and debate whether I want to trudge into the Presidio, past that welcome sign and into the long stretch of road before the entrance to Baker Beach, where the spot should be along with a bluff of a neighborhood, rows of apartment complexes, every block a half circle facing the coast. My phone shows that the neighborhood has a main road shaped like a *U*, and I begin reaching its zenith, looking for this concrete wave before sheets of rain smash me into the umbrella-less, publicly and medicinally intoxicated Oakland resident that I am. That *U* of a block is steep as hell, no spot in sight. My knees, already having traversed most of the city north–south, are aflame, begging for a break. "All for skate," I whisper to myself on some delusional *Field of Dreams* shit before I see some retaining walls that are similar to the spot in question. I even begin looking at the roofs of each building to find a pattern similar to the one backgrounding so many moments in San Francisco skate history.

Toward the bottom of the *U*, I jut into one alley and see something close but still not it. I start walking within the complex itself, going down the narrow neighborhood staircases dividing buildings and trying to not look like I'm casing the complex, when I hear the sound of urethane and ball bearings going down a hill of sorts, and in comes one kid successfully and his friend on his butt, tumbling down the driveway, laughing as he falls and mildly scrapes his knees. As they walk past me, boards in hand, one looking at the other's cell phone footage of the fall, I introduce myself and they do the same—G and O—before I show them a photo on my phone of Sean Sheffey blasting a kickflip at the spot in question circa 1995, asking them if the spot's nearby.

"We've been looking for that one too, man, and can't find it either," G says. "You know the ledges at Baker? They're just right down the hill."

"The ones with the bridge in the background," O says.

I absolutely know the ledges in question, imagining Chico Brenes ripping a backside noseblunt across the top of the biggest banks, the remnants of the Presidio's many watchtowers observing who's leaving and fleeing the San Francisco Bay, the Golden Gate Bridge looming in the background. G and O and I exchange pleasantries and goodbyes, nice kids, and I go about my way, not completing the U of the block but instead cutting back through the housing toward my original path, trying to double back into the Avenues before it gets too dark and the mountain lions stop giving a fuck and devour me like they should, displaced mammals that they are, and it's not until weeks later on a random Google Earth search that I realize I was a block off all along, that the spot is at the end of the U after all, that I started at the wrong end, and that G and O were more oblivious than I thought. But my body, continuously walking for hours now, knows nothing about this—it just knows which way is east and doesn't want to wait for a bus and lose momentum or inertia, fearing the risk of stiffening up. I walk down Clement, through all the restaurants and soft neon lights and pan-Asian pockets until I hit a bench before Arguello, in front of a diner where, I realize after regaining my breath, an ex and I first decided to become a couple, and I lie down, staring at the stars, my knees propped, my body giving labor to an unnamed exhaustion, feeling the pockets of my jacket for a light, and a few days later, still sore, I'll think, "What's the point of skate tourism if you don't even bring a board?" The physical brunt may be felt even less after a session, but I know the worst is never bearing witness to an important skate spot, a historical source, those photos taken as a teenage tourist of hubbas, that physical randomness and speculative nature of encountering space and reconfiguring your own relationship and perception of its possibility. It's about being there and seeing and feeling how your body reacts to extremely specific physical spaces, some as small as a curb cut or small wall, at a given moment, in my case in these times known as the thirties, an era when the idea of jumping down a three-stair requires a cerebral equation of velocity divided by remaining number of sick days. But here in the Bay Area there are still legendary spots visible on so many blocks, competing for space with whatever the cranes hovering over this city will soon create, vultures regenerating death into skyscrapers.

Legendary skate spots get destroyed every year; at least I can bear witness to as many of them as I can while they're here. While I'm here. Whether it's the spots or the friends with whom you've sessioned, every skateboarder, at some point, sessions with ghosts.

If he saw my shoes, curiosity would ensue. BUSENITZ, it reads across the Adidas shoe modified for the arch support, toe destruction, and lace thrashing involved in skateboarding and named after its pro endorser, San Francisco local and pro skateboarder Dennis Busenitz. A skater, Jake Phelps, board in hand, attends the same movie as me at the Castro Theatre. I caught Phelps out of the corner of my eye, hoodie with the Carhartt vest, skating on a night when I took a long walk between bouts of rain that, as evidenced by his Krooked board, didn't faze him at all. Turning toward the line after buying my ticket for the 1974 film *The Conversation* starring Gene Hackman, I look toward Phelps and see him staring right at me. I walk toward the back, inherently toward him, and give him as cool and knowing a nod as possible, something that both physicalizes recognition and recognizes gnar, and receive something between a laugh and a chuckle from Phelps, maybe shocked that people like me even believe his own projected hype or acknowledging the fact that we both know why we're looking at each other, knowing we both skate, Phelps having dedicated his life to the sport as the editor of *Thrasher* magazine from 1993 to his death in 2019. Our quasi run-in is a few months before his very publicly documented fall-to-skull-bash down Dolores Street along the city's famed Dolores Park during an unspoken but annual grassroots skate takeover of a hill Phelps would bomb alone at the crack of dawn almost daily, so comfortably that he'd document it on his phone, a fearsome act. I wonder that night at the Castro what his exit strategy will be for the evening, bombing some hill from here back toward 24th Street. I find a seat toward backstage right and see Phelps sitting toward the front center. His board drops either accidentally or very intentionally to the ground, the familiar sound a sonic boom of skateboarding recognition amid the silence of the art deco theater, devoid of the house Wurlitzer player who only plays weekends.

I was at the bottom of a massive staircase-lined hill that summitted at Taylor Street's highest point, with a gorgeous near-panoramic view of the entire north and east sides of the bay from San Francisco's North Beach/Chinatown border, when I read about Phelps's death on *Thrasher*'s Instagram, standing stunned in front of erstwhile tourists and closed shops near Grant. I had just gotten done revisiting the familiar spots of California Street—Black Rock, Pine Street bump, California gap, Cardiel Ledge, China Banks—before climbing that massive multiple-story staircase to the top of Taylor, a wall of ivy covering a chain link fence that had graced *Thrasher*'s cover in the late 1990s and early 2000s, now considered a golden era for skateboarding and the industry that profited off of dudes like Mark Gonzales or women like Elissa Steamer, willing to grind a fence and bomb two hills into oblivion, and for fools like me, playing pedestrian catch-up to their courage. Reading the news afterward, back on earth, I thought of that interaction we had or didn't have, of the times I'd seen pros like Busenitz shredding the streets solo without a care in the world, the times I've been able to bear witness. A month later, Pablo Ramirez died on 7th just before Mission Street, a fatal accident with a vehicle on a street I walked on to and from my now former job. Graffiti along the green roll-up doors and alleyways screamed his name in mourning for months, his Instagram moniker and aliases like "Jerry" spray-painted in frenetic fashion by fellow skaters who, as documented through an exploitative *San Francisco Chronicle* lens, were some of the first at the scene. I remember seeing him dancing to a vinyl DJ set spun by legend John Cardiel at 111 Minna Gallery for a Deluxe art show and skate-video premiere, the smile and joy in his eyes soundtracked and engendered by the rhythms of a man told he'd never walk again after an injury fifteen years earlier in Australia.

Phelps's glasses were encased in the concrete of Potrero del Sol Skate Park even before his death. Skaters will always remember Twin Peaks as Pablo's early morning hill-bomb spot, where he'd completed a death-defying affair by the time commuters like me were barely crossing the Bay Bridge on BART or the bus. The city will never sponsor monuments to street icons, just those heroes in privately sponsored arenas, knowing their longevity awaits upon signature of contract and for whom I sometimes cheer as well, but there is nothing more subtly coded than the language of skate spots. Of taking cabs solo to Wallows in the wee hours of dawn during a layover in Hawai'i. Of sleeping at a spot just to skate it all night. Of grimy quarters grouped together for cross-county drives and fast-food survival. In the Castro Theatre, I gawk at the opening overhead shots of San Francisco's old Union Square, its beautiful hedges lined with then-pristine concrete ledges that would later be waxed and redefine street skateboarding in the 1990s, and I wonder if—but I know—Phelps is thinking the same, with an actual memory attached to the ground, the dodged tourists, the local cops. How deeply a physical act can alter the inertia of the mind, heart, and soul and go beyond the body's capabilities and into the actualized unknown.

The four of us cram into Reuben's dark brown Cressida to head straight for downtown Los Angeles, the backdrop of every skate video, and specifically Lockwood Avenue Elementary near Los Angeles City College. Nothing was more influential than the lines street skateboarding followed from picnic table to concrete bank wave in those videos we worshipped—*Mouse, Trilogy, 20 Shot Sequence*—the expansive sound of urethane wheels echoing with the roar of ball bearings in the open, outdoor wall-less space of concrete and the gang-controlled neighborhoods surrounding it.

We all met by chance in Pomona around 1998 at Garey Park Plaza, what would later become the Sav-On ledges, a meeting ground for that era of skaters. Tony, Ray, Romeo, Reuben, and sometimes Paul started taking me downtown to the benches at Centennial Park at the end of a part of Second Street I knew well, Antique Row, full of vintage stores where we'd buy comics and toys as kids, vintage button-ups and cardigans as teens. Centennial Park, part of the Western University medical school, became our daily gym, our headquarters. We'd even meet skaters in town following bands around the southwest, like the kids from Vegas who were following Hot Water Music to the Glass House all-ages venue down the street, crashing on couches, finding spots along the way, showing us that we could do the same.

Los Angeles County is a series of villages connected by freeways. A pre-internet world of secret shows, zines, party lines, word of mouth, and skateboarding operated no differently. Seemingly invisible borders between towns become visible at the worst moments, when you give the wrong answer to *Where you from?*, and even out in the shrapnel of Los Angeles County's line in Pomona, these rules applied. It was very rare to see a skater at a spot in a bright red or baby blue shirt, Kings and Raiders gear already banned at schools along with British Knights shoes, an entire county- and district-wide gang injunction.

We park at the Jack in the Box across from Los Angeles City College. We warm up on the ledges that Rodrigo Teixeira would soon immortalize in *Menikmati*, chunky ledges that lead to a quad with a sinking five-stair, with a slanted picnic table perpetually poised as a makeshift hubba down the set. Next, we cruise forward to the long, straight handrail (now gone), at the front of the college, that made this spot a household name to every skater imagining how the hell Ed Templeton did his 50-50-to-frontside-boardslide combo here, in those

Vans no less, with a landing straight into Vermont Avenue and oncoming traffic.

We push a couple of blocks east along Lockwood Avenue until we reach the elementary school of the same name, a living place of worship for street skateboarders in a neighborhood where, if you didn't know the locals and were filming, that camera might be gone, quickly. If you were a Brown kid at Lockwood, and didn't look affiliated, and weren't around too many other white kids, and showed up at a subjectively mellow time of day, you should be good.

The trademark feature of the spot: a bank to bench with a fence backstop. This perfect concrete wave pitches you toward the fence but over the bench. When you approach the lip frontside, it's insane how much bounce and lift it gives you, but also how fast you need to go to turn that steep incline with a matched velocity and into a trick that maintains enough speed to smoothly grind across the bench and pitch body and board back into the bank without wheel bite, hanging up, or sliding out. Speed plus style equals street skateboarding. I snap a slow ollie above the bench, barely clipping into a 50-50 before sliding into the bank. Tony executes a frontside tailslide almost from jump, before spending most of the afternoon trying frontside tailslide kickflip out unsuccessfully back into the bank.

Within that split-second pop of my initial ollie, a montage of skate history flies across my mind along with the rush of not just experiencing, but realizing the experience is occurring on hallowed ground. The moment my board even touches the asphalt, I can feel the rush of being *there*, imitating Eric Koston, Tony Ferguson, Keenan Milton, Guy Mariano, Jason Dill sessioning that infamous random Los Angeles schoolyard, every song from every one of their parts filling the space between my ears: Joe Bataan's "Aftershower Funk," Herbie Hancock's "Watermelon Man," Royal Flush's "Worldwide." I can feel how the sky hovered above our heroes' heads like Koston's lines in *Las Nueve Vidas de Paco*, punch-drunk pinks and smog-induced clouds, the sky the limit for our heroes, five-hundred-dollar-a-month amateurs and pros alike who all live, film, party, and work together, some for more years than others, a soundtrack of soul classics fueling the bounce of style oozing out of this definitive era. How many times can you point to your favorite movie, the movies that you quote daily and that only other skaters know about, and say, *I was there*? Everything I land, even a kickflip on flat, feels like a Jordan buzzer beater because of the setting alone.

We hop over the nearly two-story fence and skate back to the car, somehow not towed, and hit up a couple pf spots downtown before driving back on the 60 east, getting on somewhere near the Grand Olympic where I'd just seen Rage Against the Machine play two of their last shows ever in the original formation. We talk shit on the way back about one another's weak styles and missed tricks, whether we want In-N-Out, or if we should hit up a spot on the way, maybe that white ledge at Whittier High School that only one of us could possibly grind. I keep staring in the rearview mirror at downtown's skyline, before the sound-retaining walls near the 10-60-710 interchange block the views, and we finally decide to hit up the Claremont skate park at night since it has lights. We're the only Brown kids at the park, the only kids to receive tickets from a cop who didn't apparently see the other ten kids without pads or melanin. The part that is most irritating is that our crew is too sore to skate anyway, and we're sitting down and admiring other skaters, when three officers ask for our information. I give false information out of fury at the obvious racism that I can't articulate at fifteen but can feel staring back at me. I tear up that ticket when I get home and throw it away. The guilt sets in immediately. I dive back into the garbage, find the ticket, tape it together, and confess my nonexistent-but-existent crime. My dad has to take off work and get harangued by a judge in front of me, red in the face, yelling at us both, threatening me with juvie time. "How could you lie?!" the judge demands to know. Then and now I want to reply: Because your officers were lazy. Because it was biased, four Brown kids from Pomona in Claremont at any time of day, because there is a meth epidemic hitting the Inland Empire and this is how your officers spend their Sunday evening. Because if this were San Francisco, they might've planted hubba on all of us before lawfully discharging their weapons. These are the daydreams of a fifteen-year-old Brown skateboarder. I get grounded for months, largely for getting even remotely close to the criminal justice system. It's a harsh lesson to realize that no matter how high my grades are, fucking up like this takes all precedence, putting me and my parents in the crosshairs of a judge's wrath, the cost of one of the greatest, most legendary sessions I've ever had, of touching the mount from which the holy sermon of Los Angeles skateboarding is told, before one man determined who among us criminals deserved the crime.

14th and Jackson

When I talk to people in the city about whether they come to Oakland, be it 2007 or 2019, the answer is a resounding "never," followed by redundant stories of car break-ins and not wanting to take BART at night. No matter how many East Bay, Marin and Contra Costa County, or Central Valley residents head through the Transbay tunnel or across the Golden Gate or Bay Bridge every day to San Francisco, going to Oakland is a seemingly annual trip for city dwellers, who usually make the pilgrimage for city-sponsored art crawls or like-minded Fox Theater concerts or, at one time, a Warriors game. The lack of streetlights and noticeable foot traffic for years made people fear downtown Oakland compared to the more geographically concentrated city by the bay. Despite the similar amount of crime in the two cities, it's Oakland where everyone assumes they'll be shot on sight or that the ghost of Huey Newton will greet them at the 12th Street BART with a shotgun and a toll for Whites Only.

Downtown Oakland is changing in many ways, but my habits on 14th and Jackson aren't one of them. A smoke by Lake Merritt and some quarter snacks from the bodega next to the Ruby Room lead to nuggets from the fast-food dispensary next to my old building, Peralta Apartments on 13th and Jackson. Eating and smoking under the ground-floor tree, three floors below the apartment that housed me, my books, my desk, my box spring, and mattress twice the box spring's size beginning in June 2007, a year after I graduated from UC Berkeley a few BART stops away.

Downtown was feared when I first moved to the East Bay in 2002. Most businesses were pursuing the supposed golden ticket of a 415 area code and San Francisco zip code. Aside from Clorox, the Warriors, and Kaiser, it was the small businesses of 17th Street's previously tree-lined lane between Franklin and Webster and Chinatown that held up downtown for years, most of the money leaving around 2:00 p.m. when the business class went home early or the morning spots closed and what few dives remained didn't entertain the Lafayette clientele. Vacant lots and dilapidated car repair shops dotted Telegraph across from the Oakland Black Box, where I first performed poetry in the Town as a teenager.

Not much met the eye when I first arrived, but downtown had the daytime businesses that occasionally extended their hours for locals on the weekends: The deli on 14th and Franklin that closed at the end of 2019. Mama Buzz Cafe on Telegraph and 23rd, whose staff also published the literary magazine *Kitchen Sink*, the older writers and poets sneaking us into their twenty-one-and-over open mics advertised in the back of those magazines, printed on recycled paper by one of the several presses still around in Ghost Town or West Oakland.

From my window, I'd look west toward Broadway across the mostly empty parking lot housing the USPS trucks across the street from the downtown post office on the Alice Street side of the lot. At night between trucks, the homeless would find shelter or twenty-somethings like me would sneak a piss in between bars or dates. A shin-high ledge lined the lot where the local derelicts would sip and smoke atop the white streaks of goose and egret shit dropped from trees housing entire aviaries downtown. At night the sound of the birds mating and fighting fills the blocks up and down Oak near the 11th Street tunnel and the Oakland Museum all the way up to 14th Street. It's from this third-floor window that I spotted an old couch—an abandoned brown, leather, three-seater beaut lurking by the hardware emporium on Alice and 12th—that my roommate and I dragged a few blocks, then up a couple of flights to my four-hundred-and-change room inside apartment 310. A low, sprawling tree on the eastern Jackson Street side of the lot, closer to my window, provided a fleeting shaded relief that summer, the tree roots bursting through the asphalt lot that, over the years, more and more people paid to park in during business hours for nearby court sessions or marriage license appointments at the Alameda County courthouse, the iconic Gotham building from which the Black Panthers proclaimed their platform while facing the lake.

We inherited the three-bedroom apartment from college friends, all of us previous undergraduate coopers used to one another's habits. In common was our shared home state and the unspoken boundaries of our debauchery. Hourly San Francisco Financial District temp wages and the academic tutoring equivalent at nearby Laney College fueled our livelihoods. I subsisted on fast food next door and the taco truck on the other side of the lake, skateboarding across a preconstruction 14th Street with potholes and graveled nascent bike lanes before ollieing up as thick a sidewalk as I would have wallriding Rome's Colosseum, let alone East Oakland's Coliseum. Lake Merritt's sidewalk was getting paved, starting at the columns near Lakeshore, signs of gentrification slowly emerging with the economy plummeting as quickly as full-time job prospects. I'd sit on my board on the east side of the lake or on the white benches on East 18th if they weren't covered with too much bird shit, smashing carne asada quesadillas and Mexican Coca-Colas, not knowing that in 2019 I'd propose to my wife on the side of the lake closest to the now-renovated 14th Street.

The bodega heads that still own the organic grocery on the ground floor of Hilltop Apartments, a towering downtown art deco building on Jackson, knew us so well we got free bottles on our birthdays on the way out of the bar next door. We knew the bartenders and when they worked. If we didn't have to work for the day, we were at the lake, or lurking in Chinatown, or just home, in my case, writing a play with a faint chance of production. No coffee, French presses, fresh fruit, dinners made at home. It was mostly black liquor-store bags, a modicum of groceries, lentils as entrées. My vinyl collections were more preserved than my dietary choices. We played Stones, Velvet Underground, glam Bowie, Beatles, and Murder City Devils records in their entirety, with Turner Classic Movies on mute, the TV's sound turned on only for ritualized *Seinfeld* or *Twilight Zone* viewings after the bar.

Clean Skateshop was still on Franklin near 15th, its indoor miniramp the training ground for two young boys donning turbans and shredding those afternoons I'd go in for new bearings and the latest *Thrasher*. We went on dates, i.e., got drinks with girls who somehow stayed over, unfortunately bearing witness to my existence. When I did have temp jobs, I spent my time reading plays online, keeping my mind active, the equivalent of a hooper going to sleep with his eyes open and a basketball in his hands. Still, folks enjoyed being over. Odd watch parties for post-We-Believe-era Warriors games, even a hand-drawn bracket for the 2008 NBA Playoffs. We hosted a viewing party when Caltrans shut down the eastern expanse of the Bay Bridge, building the temporary S-shaped, slow-speed detour at the westbound entrance of Treasure Island that fascinated us Los Angeles freeway-series transplants.

"Temporal" as a lifestyle was an understatement. Many a random road trip started from the meters in front of the building on 13th Street, facing east and tempting us to head in the same direction on 80. Irresponsibility is almost intrinsic to that early-twenties era when the taste of the cheapest draft residually lingers and the feeling of economic security is a fleeting concept inappropriate for the times. Odd now, weighing that era of barely making the four-hundred-dollar rent against being the bottom-rung gentrifiers of our time, if only for having college degrees, but we awoke to the reality of the recession—no jobs, no future—every day for what would be years.

It's been thirteen years since I woke up to a crime scene, and there is still no plaque honoring Chauncey Bailey, the *Oakland Post* journalist shot and killed on 14th just before Alice Street in the early morning hours of August 2, 2007. An improvised memorial was generated at the base of a nearby tree. Paid muscle from Your Black Muslim Bakery, under investigation by Bailey for accusations of extortion, racketeering, and human trafficking, assassinated Bailey. The pursuit of Bailey's murderers was markedly slow until a group of investigative journalists, active and retired, revealed connections between Your Black Muslim Bakery's owner and the very Oakland police leading the murder investigation. The exposed collusion prompted then OPD chief Wayne Tucker to resign and led to the subsequent arrest of Yusuf Bey IV. A recent effort by Oakland City Council member Lynette Gibson McElhaney to place a memorial plaque honoring Bailey was promised and then delayed in October 2019, partly due to plans to expand the scope of the memorial. The construction on 14th between Alice and Jackson remains ongoing, and there is no timetable as of writing for Bailey's memorial plaque or otherwise defined object.

Just over a year after Bailey's murder, this intersection was flooded with rage in the wake of Oscar Grant III's murder by BART police on New Year's Day 2009. Mayor

Ron Dellums nonviolently parted a sea of protestors here on 14th and Jackson before addressing a crowd rightfully demanding justice for the unarmed, handcuffed, and executed man shot and killed on the southbound Fruitvale Station platform in East Oakland. As the protests turned into minor riots, the owner of the Ruby Room bar, synonymous with the Oakland-based motorcycle club East Bay Rats, stood outside his bar, shotgun in hand, ready for the type of looting that generally occurred a few blocks west of Jackson toward the bus stops on 14th and Broadway, at the then Foot Locker next to Pizza Man (also gone) and the still-existing hair store a couple more blocks up Telegraph Avenue. I had already moved a half joint away from Peralta to a studio on 17th and Madison and joined the demonstration after work. While 14th and Broadway is the unspoken meeting ground for demonstrations due to its proximity to city hall, the question of where the demonstrations go when night comes is the question. The night of the marches, I demonstrated with coworkers-slash-activists, friends who taught youth by day and risked arrest at night. The later the night, the closer the overtime cops approached. I turned around and saw some friends being arrested and others fleeing east toward the lake, rendezvousing near the then-standing Merchants Parking toward Webster. I fled to Berkeley just before the calls poured in on my thick flip phone about a police car aflame on my corner, assuredly the same cop I'd seen in my rearview.

New residents and developers alike no longer speak of downtown but instead use Google Maps–influenced terms to distinguish new from old, supposed safety from projected violence, those with money from those without. Or they use the new city-sponsored term "Oakland Central" that's slapped on trash cans along Broadway and on branded windbreaker jackets worn by the new security sentries walking purposelessly around downtown. Nothing feels curated for people who do Oakland things, like occupy 14th and Broadway when the Warriors win, who enjoyed marijuana before it was a new investment vertical. Nothing screams *I'm happy to be here* more than new citizenry walking their dogs downtown in noise-and-culture-canceling Bluetooth headphones. At night, police park their unattended cars with sirens flashing for hours near 13th and Broadway to deter any type of public congregation in front of DeLauer's newsstand or those few Black-owned clubs on the 400 block of 14th Street, which have complained for years about intimidation tactics and shakedowns from OPD, repealing liquor and cabaret licenses seemingly at their discretion.

A California Historical Landmark plaque will be installed inside the lobby of the new high-rise on 13th and Franklin, replacing Merchants Parking Garage, noting that the city block was the original location of the University of California. Imagine if every new skyscraper had a plaque for the many small businesses that its existence helped close, those businesses that were promised foot traffic but instead closed up shop from the escalation of rent, never seeing those nouveau-riche residents in their stores who ask the price before walking out and saying to their friends, *I could get this on Amazon for*—. The previously commissioned Warriors murals along the wall of the Marriott and the team's former practice facility on the top floor have already been painted over since the team moved to San Francisco. Not surprising, since the City of Oakland's arts commission has been suspended since 2011, draining the Town of a decade's worth of artistic potential. I remember all these histories and what local markers of their existence remain as I stare at the black tarp covering six or seven stories' worth of new housing, the billion-dollar phrase that so far has meant "no affordable housing." When I stare at a new condo, I wonder where the contractors' offices are and whether they're local, and I wonder whether the predominantly Brown hands building the structures are local. Which of these many construction workers will move into one of the units they are building between here, San Francisco, San Jose, Fresno, Tracy, and Stockton? The cranes tasked with building a new skyline became the majority at the start of 2018, and it's odd seeing professionals in new boots having cigarette breaks in front of their nameless converted mechanic's shops turned corporate headquarters. The top floor of our old building was entirely Section 8 and I'm curious whether it still is, whether the new building on the other side of Jackson will be, what percentage of either will be affordable in a Bay Area where six figures is increasingly defined as "low income" in the eyes of banks, investors, loan dealers, and all those professional evaluators of wealth and analytically derived concepts of self.

The day before I leave Oakland for practically anywhere that isn't San Francisco or Berkeley, my anxiety propels me downtown toward Lake Merritt, a type of travel anxiety pushing me straight to the axis of both the city and my life circumnavigating it, reconnecting through physical proximity to something tangible and memorable before anything, everything, goes astray the moment I cross the Altamont Pass. During panic attacks, my entire back would curl into violent punctuation marks while I drove, forcing me to pull off the road and into urgent care those first few years I lived here, dealing with the self emerging each morning in the fogged mirror of this apartment. Most days downtown were cerebral hazes in which my body would somehow appear in Amtrak seats at Jack London, facing and watching commuters pass through in the middle of the afternoon to the Central Valley in one direction and Sacramento in the other, allowing time to progress without contributing much other than worry and journal pages toward a play that, somehow, received a grant and got produced a year later. It was here, downtown, that managing anxiety meant mitigating rather than abstaining from shit routines and creating complementary productive practices that have turned the most tumultuous tides into a daily metastasized existence in my thirties.

However much I've evolved alongside it, when the anxiety hits, find me walking in circles through the ground-dug circular labyrinth near the end of Staten, a miniature version of the labyrinth at Sibley Volcanic Regional Preserve above the Caldecott Tunnel. It's illogical and consuming and makes my palms sweat on Sundays when the intrinsic sewer smell mixes with fresh bay breezes on the estuary side of the lake, toward Adams Point. The estuary islands nearby appear a running jump away, they're so deceptively close to the shore, and I remember an ongoing debate with friends about whether canoeing out to the islands and camping amid the egrets' cacophonous filth is physically and ethically possible.

I frequently encounter silent racism when I'm standing

around in random public places, particularly as a larger human with brown skin; nouveau city dwellers are put off by the cultural challenge of seeing an otherwise beatnik do hippie shit as a form of reclamation in the middle of Oakland and *not* be white. Again anxiety, but also that self-consciousness of leaving a space that's becoming increasingly more expensive, more laborious, increasingly inhumane, with fewer families, fewer kids, more homelessness, more aculturalist tendencies replacing historical narratives, more sprawling commutes on "last call" tech shuttles leaving the Central Valley for San Francisco or Tesla's factory in Fremont. Amid work, the sardined commutes, the constant reports of realtors' dollars flooding lobbying campaigns throughout the state, solace meets resistance when I'm standing around downtown and bearing witness, remembering and documenting the befores and my place within its breathing afters.

If the Bay Area is a microcosm, six figures and stock options will become the base level for surviving in America. Some of the marquee names here are already planning their move away from downtown Oakland and to their founders' midwestern hometowns. Square took up first residential digs here, leasing the bulk of the former Sears building after Uber backed out, while Lyft opened a West Oakland facility at the end of Grand Avenue, and

Kaiser, founded in Oakland in 1945, is currently building a sprawling new downtown headquarters behind the
Paramount on Broadway westward toward Grand and
Telegraph. The kind of anxiety my wife and I shared
the night news broke of the Sears building being sold to
Uber—we were either so shocked or so drunk that we
still can't remember the name of the bar where we were.
When we visited friends in Portland in the months after
the announcement, we imagined the possibility of living
somewhere that hadn't been colonized by Spain, somewhere that wasn't California.

I channeled this worry into a script for a short film,
Payday, about a day in the life of an aspiring Oakland artist trying to get a major grant check during the day and
go on a date at night. A young tutor commutes from the
East Bay all the way to San Francisco and gets stood up
for a morning appointment by affluent parents who de-
liver a very belated cancellation via text. The tutor heads
back, unpaid, to their home in Oakland for a coffee and
smoke break with a friend at Lincoln Square Park, aka
Chinatown Park, the one with the basketball courts that
start on 11th and Harrison, before going back to the city
again in the afternoon to get their paycheck from their
second job as a temp worker in San Francisco's Financial
District. Half the reason I wrote this was to get an establishing shot from behind the characters showing the

whole scene in the park—the dragon swing set, the basketball courts and constant pickup games, downtown Oakland's skyline, the playground—with the Tribune Tower perfectly placed in the background. The protagonist ultimately has to go back to the city again for their paycheck, chasing down a surprisingly cordial CPA on MUNI at Forest Hill Station, the oldest subway station west of the Mississippi. It's a film that ideally would showcase the types of adventures and interactions that are gone now in an optimized Bay, cloud-driven metrics and returns on investment dictating everything from the way we get paid and the way we make love to the way we buy homes.

Before the script was even done, I got the shot without actors in place, two Chinatown locals instead sitting on the red metal and curved-back benches in the corner facing the dragon and the courts where my roommates and I tripped acid for the first time, frequently smoked, and utilized the space as a de facto meeting ground at night. I heard the Merchants parking lot was being destroyed for a new development that will become the tallest Oakland has seen. I didn't know that it'd be an even closer city-block-sized development that'd jeopardize the shot, even when I was recording background audio near the sign explaining the history of the dragon boat, the sound of basketballs, kids playfully screaming in multiple languages, the AC Transit stop on the corner and its multiple necessary lines to East Oakland, the sounds of the Town playing in the new shadows of skyscraper investments.

I wrote *Payday* imagining that the extras would be reflective of the mid-aughts Oakland I'd moved to and that the film is an homage to: when the social, facial-surveillance archiving on mobile phones hadn't come into play yet; when our minds were still building MySpace albums conceptually out of our CVS-lab-developed photos of road trips taken with printed-out MapQuest directions. The lead character awakens in a slightly better version of my East Oakland studio circa 2010, the script projecting my still-aflame self-determined *I live here to make art here* vibe. The character is also inspired by my friend Isa, born and raised in Oakland, who not only shares an abbreviated version of my sister's name but who says I remind them of their own brother. They moved away to the Philippines to live with their mother, another piece of this Oakland film that was gone before we rolled tape.

Maybe it's for the best. A sign of the California times to bury that part of me that, at age sixteen, road-tripped up north, crashed at my sister's co-ops, and lurked around Oakland and the city, figuring it all out on pre-digital BART tickets. Nowadays, the proverb I used to tell everyone younger than me—to live alone in a city once in your life—is as cliché as the concept of pulling oneself up by the bootstraps. Cities are increasingly turning into dormitory solutions, personal space, like public space, disappearing and constrained. A sign to bury the part of me that will always believe people should move to cities or states or farmlands to contribute to them rather than to impose their own set of acultural norms and as fair-weather commitments to the proverbial, diminishing community.

But who am I in the grand scheme of things, and how dry am I compared to the amount of swagger the pimps and gators and Towers of Power had over the years? These words will never re-create the Oakland reflected in the swish of Hammer's parachute pants or the dread of Loma Prieta's tremors. I still feel scorn watching the Malonga Casquelord Center for the Arts murals get covered by new developments, even though city funding was allocated for the murals' creation. Culture isn't just taking a back seat; it's a hostage in the back seat of city government's priorities.

Whether or not *Payday* will ever happen, I suppose it's already in a suspended type of production with my shot of the Tribune. Sometimes I watch the footage in color, in black and white, as a still, as a loop. The playback generates more questions than answers about an

Oakland I know better than the eastern Los Angeles County sprawl that raised me.

How can I tell you how much an intersection means to me—Warriors victories and simultaneous unspoken citywide agreements to protest here, memories of friends getting arrested and fights ensuing and tear gas being thrown—without sounding pedantic, soapbox driven, as if having an opinion is the equivalent of publicly bearing a contagious disease, a cog in the path to your next call? I want Oakland to first be associated with the Panthers rather than the Raiders, with an animal that protects and contributes rather than a figure that plunders and departs, and with schools that are public and not chartered into foreclosed futures for the minds of kids, as we've seen happen in the last decade.

In the final weeks of 2019, these memories whirl around me as cars maintain their evergreen multiple-file entry lines into the fast-food drive-thru before noon. The last Raiders home game ever starts in about an hour, the franchise having decided to leave Oakland again, this time for a massive new Las Vegas arena across the street from the now infamous Mandalay Bay hotel and casino. The Coliseum will host its final Raider Nation tailgate, its final fight, arrest, the final day of the decades-deep Black Hole.

Win or lose, the Coliseum's packed with silver and

black every year, fans ready to rep a culture where *cholos* with their kids go arm in arm with gorilla-costumed diehards in spiked vests. Imagine a masquerade ball from hell sponsored by Bud Light and soundtracked by Too Short. Feared and envied worldwide, the Nation takes over Southwest Airlines every weekend, flying in for home games from all across the West Coast. But also imagine a tailgate bigger than most city swap meets, where friends from across state and family lines set up shop, shoot the dozens, and truly find community in the middle of a parking lot where season ticket passes are handed down to next of kin. There's something so authentically weird, goth, funky, tough-guy-turned-cosplayer about the Raiders culture, one that may be exported outside California but will always be linked to the Town.

What will the internally displaced Raider Nation do now every Sunday morning before 1:00 p.m. kickoff? At least the move to Los Angeles was within state lines. The Bo Jackson era seeded the idea that Raider Nation is a concept, a psychology, that becomes a physical, actualized force on Sundays and is demarcated by Coliseum parking lot numbers that have been crew identifiers for generations. After the years the Raiders spent playing in the Los Angeles Coliseum, my cousins, like many Angelenos, started making the drive up to Oakland as many weekends as possible, and in this last season "to kiss the ground" one last time before the Vegas era begins.

Is the Oakland Coliseum the next space to disappear?

The Athletics continue to lobby for a new waterfront, made-for-baseball stadium near the already tourist-primed Jack London Square, while pitching turning the Coliseum into a multiuse retail, housing, and public-park complex. It has all the amenities necessary—a subway stop, an Amtrak station, a subway shuttle directly to the airport, bay views of San Francisco's and Oakland's skylines—but it's located in East Oakland, which is service deprived and perpetually stigmatized. Given housing prices in the Bay Area, will the Coliseum embody its namesake by becoming a massive encampment, housing those members of Raider Nation displaced not just from fanfare but from housing? Visions and thoughts of the future swirl before me, the honks of impatient horns blaring nearby at the automated fast-food beeline.

And I'm still here, somewhat sober and still eating too many fries in the developing shade of a new six-story building that's replacing the root-bursting dead asphalt that housed those derelicts, the bird shit, the mail trucks, the "empty" fluid spaces increasingly disappearing in downtown Oakland.

Still—What do I fear forgetting? Fear losing? The ability to walk around the lake and point to my former roof and say, "Everyday I'd start the day *there*"?—is Lake Merritt the last thing I want to see, ever? As if having this choice is something life and Oakland permit.

I've lived in the East Bay for over half my life. I've stubbornly believed Oakland was the only city that made me want to be myself. It wasn't until 2019 that I questioned that belief. And reaffirmed my answer.

And why a place, and not a person, a scent, a touch, a song, knowing full well the lake, too, is man-made? I wonder if I'm mistaking these walls and Lake Merritt and Chinatown's alleys and the subway elevating toward Fruitvale for the smiles, sweat, laughter, drink orders, inside jokes, and apartment buzzer numbers of old friends now breathing and living on other sides of this still-spinning axis. For the hope that the faces that are still here will not just remain but flourish. This persistent fear, acceptance, and forecast of change guides my fingers to the shutter button and pen, documenting all the same. It is December 2019 in the city of Oakland, my habits are not changing, and I no longer live in the downtown Oakland of 2007 or in the downtown deemed Uptown or Oakland Central. Why yell at people on the train when I can show them a hi-res still image of that unobstructed angle of the Tribune Tower and, in an all-caps Sharpie caption, scream, DOES ANY-ONE ELSE MISS THOSE RED LETTERS IN OAKLAND'S SKYLINE, TOO?

Post

An Afterworld

If the essays in this book are the thematic seams, or fault lines, connecting California, then the COVID-19 pandemic, police violence, and 2020's record-breaking California fire season grabbed and pulled at those seams as hard, quickly, and destructively as possible.

The events detailed in the preceding essays, and the ability to physically traverse the state of California, took place between 2015 and the beginning months of 2020, with the first near-final draft submitted to my editor in April 2020, about a month after California, like the entire country, began to shelter in place. Businesses shut down and layoffs steadily and then rapidly increased.

It's no understatement to say that I am writing this afterword in a post-COVID world—one where nearly 200,000 Americans, and nearly 900,000 worldwide, have died from this ongoing disease. To date, 14,000

Californians have died from the disease. There are currently over 760,000 active COVID-19 cases in California.

My contract copywriting gig for an in-person live software-tutorial show went thankfully fully remote, many of my coworkers assuming we'd return to our office in the city in June, assuming that the infection curve would subside to a glacial rate, before realizing that this is the country that voted 2016 into office, before watching whatever progress made in the state of California evaporate by Memorial Day weekend and every climate-change-exacerbated summer holiday to date.

We've just passed Labor Day and the federal government has only given citizens $1,200 since the spring to survive. There has been no national day of mourning, reflection, or other tribute to the massive amount of loss of human life, no condolences from our current executive administration. An average of 1 million Americans a week have applied for federal assistance, and as of August 2020, nearly 20 million Americans are left hanging, relying on solely state-directed aid to survive. Crowdsourcing and GoFundMe campaigns have become Band-Aids for a fragmented, broken system of government aid during a global crisis. Federal unemployment assistance in the form of weekly six-hundred-dollar payments has dried up, with Congress going on summer recess while millions of Americans without work try to figure out how they're going to survive.

People are hungry, without work, and increasingly without homes. Moratoriums on evictions have reached all levels of government, but whatever is not paid now will be expected to be paid to landlords, by whoever's hand, come the pandemic's end. In numerous places across town a Town Fridge has popped up, a grassroots, free, grab-and-go, healthy-food-distribution network operated through public and volunteer-managed refrigerators across Oakland, with like-minded efforts in New York and Los Angeles. A June 2020 report noted that in the past year, the number of homeless residents in Los Angeles alone jumped from forty thousand to over sixty thousand, according to the Los Angeles Homeless Services Authority. In lieu of federal relief, eviction moratoriums are extended month to month in an odd homage to most Americans' paycheck (and revenue-generation) cycles.

Despite the San Francisco Board of Supervisors' unanimous approval of emergency powers for Mayor London Breed to seize 8,250 hotel rooms for seven thousand vulnerable homeless people, she did nothing, allowing the April 26, 2020, deadline to pass and openly making statements she refused to follow through on. The city had previously acquired two thousand rooms, and over the summer months, with COVID infection rates rising, Mayor Breed only secured six hundred additional rooms by August before she stopped acquiring shelter-in-place hotel rooms at all. Instead, group shelters, where COVID rates could skyrocket, as happened in the infamous Moscone Center shelters at the start of the pandemic, are the city's proposed method to attend to its unhoused populations amid a pandemic. At the state level, the California Supreme Court refused to hear challenges to Proposition C passed by voters in 2018, unlocking half a billion dollars of funds previously earmarked for homeless programs in San Francisco.

Exacerbating the pandemic and California's housing crisis is this year's wildfire season and the new element of lightning. In August, over ten thousand lightning strikes in less than a week have generated over 350 individual fires, forcing tens of thousands of Californians to evacuate. This includes the massive SCU Lightning Complex Fire, a nearly four-hundred-thousand-acre fire spreading from the hills east of Santa Clara and San Jose all the way into the Joaquin Valley, and the LNU Lightning Complex Fire in Napa, Sonoma, and Yolo Counties and more, encircling all of Lake Berryessa just north of the Bay Area and nearly the same size as the SCU fires.

North of these fires in Mendocino, the massive

August Complex Fire, the largest in California history, rages across nearly 1 million acres and at roughly 30 percent containment as of writing. Massive fires are destroying historic sites at Big Basin along the coast, forcing evacuations in the Santa Cruz Mountains. The ongoing Creek Fire is destroying the Sierra Nevada between Yosemite and Kings Canyon on the outskirts of Fresno County, with helicopters airlifting survivors standing in lakes trying to avoid being set aflame. Similar rescue efforts are happening near Lake Oroville and the city of Paradise, a town destroyed by the 2018 Camp Fire with over eighty-five deaths, in the wake of the North Complex Fire just over 250,000 acres large and at 30 percent containment as of writing. One of the closest fires to my hometown is the Bobcat Fire, traversing the San Gabriel foothills from Arcadia to the High Desert and Antelope Valley, nearly destroying the legendary Mount Wilson Observatory from which the majority of our radio transmissions have been broadcast since we were kids, the smoke connecting with that of the El Dorado and Apple Fires burning east of San Bernardino.

All the California fires mentioned in the essays in this book have been topped in terms of size, strength, and economic impact by the unprecedented wildfire season of 2020. From eastern Washington State through

Oregon, where, as of writing, nearly 10 percent of the state's population has been evacuated, from California's northernmost counties to the bottom of Southern California's Imperial Valley, the United States west of the Rockies is on fire amid a pandemic.

There are currently over 1,300 incarcerated prisoners across 113 incarcerated teams fighting fires alongside Cal Fire and county agencies, less than the two hundred teams Cal Fire can usually deploy, but COVID infections in prisons have limited the number of prisoners available to be deployed. The demand for firefighters has forced California governor Newsom's hand on signing legislation that allows prisoners to apply for firefighting jobs post-release, jobs that many are already executing at extremely high levels. Still, the pipeline to employment has many strings attached and limitations and is not a blanket acceptance of all prisoners for job eligibility.

With fires raging near large prisons across the state, the incarcerated across California and Oregon are detailing inhumane conditions, consumed by heat, smoke inhalation, and nonexistent PPE. Transferring prisoners from one facility to another, even after COVID outbreaks were detected among staff and inmates alike, increased infections across the state's prison systems. A transfer of male prisoners from Chino to San Quentin led to an immediate outbreak. Leaked prisoner testimonies on social media tell similar stories: being told "good luck" by guardsmen and having only a single mask weeks into the pandemic.

In mid-August, the hills off River Road near Salinas, Chualar, Spreckels, and Gonzales in the Salad Bowl are ablaze, amid a statewide heat wave, in what's currently known as the River Fire and its western neighbor, the Carmel Fire. Collectively, those two fires cover nearly fifty thousand acres just west of where I drove around, where Abuelo once irrigated the crops. Now gray smoke is flooding the Salad Bowl, looming over predominantly undocumented workers who are masked against both COVID and the smoke, if they are lucky. The smoke exacerbates the housing crises facing the most vulnerable, always the undocumented laborers living, in the case of East Salinas, five families to a house, barely making ends meet. How do people quarantine safely in such conditions? The answer, *THEY DON'T*, is screamed at those who are conscious of the hands harvesting for, but not profiting from, coastal farm-to-table dietary lifestyles.

When grassroots relief efforts reached the Salinas Valley, the farmworkers requested school supplies for their kids to help them adjust to remote classrooms and distance learning. A viral photo shows two young

Brown girls in the parking lot of a Taco Bell using the restaurant's internet to connect to their virtual classes. According to a Pew Research study, over 80 percent of white households own laptops, compared to only 57 percent of Latino households. A different study indicated that only 40 percent of Latino households in America have access to Wi-Fi. Activists turned grassroots non-profits accept funds through digital-cash apps to buy those school supplies that the farmworkers can't afford, let alone N95 masks to combat the smoke from the fires and masks necessary to combat COVID-19. Imagine wearing two masks amid hellfire's brimstone and knowing your kids aren't secure, that they're alone in a parking lot trying to connect to opportunity.

For the most vulnerable, the evergreen frontline worker, the conditions are drastically worse than the worse. The many undocumented Americans who contribute billions in labor to the nation's economy are not eligible for any of the emergency services or benefits. This is the broad swath of citizens and undocumented workers alike at the bottom of the wage-for-existence economic hierarchy. However increasingly "frontline" these workers become, they return home from work to overpopulated housing, exacerbating COVID's potential to spread. Unions reported inconsistent distribution of PPE, hand sanitizer, and other preventative measures in

California fields. Undocumented farmworkers are in dire need of PPE, with many prioritizing school supplies and resources for their kids over their own needs in the fields.

And despite the wealth of the Golden State, housing opportunities are slim. Prices are still skyrocketing amid a pandemic. Senate Bill 1120, potentially historic state legislation that would have helped redefine California's ability to build duplexes on single-family-house lots regardless of their zoning, died after the time for it to pass on the state floor ran out, a remarkable failure considering how difficult and expensive it is to build any type of housing, affordable or market rate, and more remarkable still that such a modest reform, single to duplex (a step down from the fourplex-advocating legislation of the bill's failed predecessor, Senate Bill 50), would not be urgently fast-tracked in the state capitol.

The murder of Breonna Taylor, the killing of George Floyd recorded on video, and the resurfaced attention to Elijah McClain's 2019 killing, all at the hands of well-armed police officers, led to the most recent and most massive iteration of the Black Lives Matter movement. Currently the Department of Justice has arrested over three hundred people in new sweeps aimed at "wiping out" alleged "members" of this deregulated organization. For many, the first months of the pandemic were a balancing act of social-distancing measures and mass demonstrations domestically and abroad. Even smaller towns in California, like Norco, had Black Lives Matter protests met with counterprotestors; across the country, this led to increasingly violent and lethal confrontations, such as the murders of Joseph Rosenbaum and Anthony M. Huber in Kenosha, Wisconsin, by an illegally armed, teenage, white male terrorist.

Many cities are debating defunding their police departments and reallocating resources toward nonviolence, nonpolice solutions, and community investment. San Francisco's and Oakland's school boards severed ties with their police forces by summer—with Oakland's legislation, the George Floyd Resolution to Eliminate the Oakland Schools Police Department, taking back over $2 million from OPD to put toward student services—with local colleges following suit.

In July 2020, the Oakland City Council approved the commemorative renaming of 14th Street between Oak Street and Broadway Avenue as Chauncey Bailey Way, after the murdered *Oakland Post* journalist. Some call it Frank Ogawa Plaza, others Oscar Grant Jr. Plaza, but the protests are centered there all the same, on the northwest corner of Broadway and 14th Street. During one of the daily Black Lives Matter protests in downtown Oakland, two federal agents were shot and killed by far-right conspiracy theorists hoping the protestors would be blamed. Also this summer, the racist killer of Nia Wilson—the transgender eighteen-year-old attacked and killed in a 2018 hate crime at Oakland's MacArthur BART station—was sentenced in July to life in prison without parole. The nearly two-year-long public vigil on the platform's lower entrance level was a chilling reminder of the threats posed to trans communities of color in the wake of Black Lives Matter and the larger corporatization of Pride events in the city, the closures of queer clubs, and the need for trans-directed nonprofits and greater trans rights.

Amid all this, and as local businesses board and shut their doors and bank on state and local relief, Mayor Libby Schaaf cast a historic tie-breaking vote against a modest $3 million reallocation of police funds to Oakland's new mental health response pilot, the Department of Violence Prevention's work with youth services, and more non-police-related forms of deescalation. This reallocation of funds was considered a conservative reform compared to larger cuts proposed by other councilmembers. Still, Schaaf voted against the bill in a rarely seen tiebreaker vote, despite numerous citizens being in favor of full defunding or, at least, the larger cuts proposed in a separate bill. Sacramento followed suit, voting against larger police reforms later that summer with AB 1506, which passed modest reforms to already internationally denounced chokehold tactics while failing to prevent repeatedly abusive police officers from keeping their badges.

I have been trying to find hope amid chaos in the days and nights when the hours shrink to fingers around my neck and I can hear every part of ancestral, textbook, and experiential histories shaking me awake. And it's fine, because I'm under a roof and there's no guilt in that, or in existing, here at least. The surreal and illogical is the everyday. As a freelance reporter, lately I've been trying to find those out there generating hope through their own socially distanced engagements with society. I don't know who I am most days other than myself. We do the immediate buying of the now short-supplied essentials like toilet paper and cleaning products, as well as whatever gloves and hand sanitizer we can get for ourselves. My fiancée and I quickly came to the realization that our June wedding was probably in jeopardy. But we did get married, a virtual ceremony hosted by Alameda County, and I overhear her in online video work meetings describing me as "my husband," and the adjustment isn't out of the ordinary. It's a change in an indoors that remains physically the same amid the chaos in the skies outside—gifts for a wedding that never alchemized and signs of balancing professional intrusions with domestic sanity. My lungs have blossomed in such a way that even when I was smoking in bars in the nation's capital seven nights a week they didn't feel nearly quite as snug a sting. An injection-to-the-spine type of tingle. The air quality reads GOOD tonight in green on private and government websites alike.

It's September 2020 and the summer is now gone like Stevie warned us about in 1976 on *Songs in the Key of Life*. I wake up, read the news as best as rationally possible, drink the coffee, and do the things, as an increasingly thick glass museum display case appears in whatever room I sit, figuratively holding previous visions of myself and my previous everyday captive. No more commuting here and there with a joint half-lit in my lips or that burning, running sensation in my calf pushing more so than walking down the street. I was initially on this vampire routine of only skating at night at Safeway, and when too many unmarked cars kept passing through, I started doing the early morning routines at Rockridge BART, finally learning the ollie-less slappy grinds heavily associated with the parking lot's well-waxed curbs. My body's adjusted to not having a happy hour full of crosstown walks interrupted by French fries, beers, and pre-rolls all digested between work and home. I don't miss rush-hour commutes, but I miss riding the train; the data shows that it's healthier than some commuters' own homes in terms of preventing COVID or spreading infection. Rims of public basketball hoops have been knobbed with two-by-fours or simply unscrewed by city parks and rec departments to prevent social congregation. There's sand in skate parks. Meals are made later in the day, the refrain of time being a nonexistent, relative term fully accepted now in a work-from-home, stay-at-home society. I use the box of unused wedding invitation envelopes to prop up my quasi-ergonomic work-from-home scenario from the pandemic's start to the end of summer, freelancing marketing and writing gigs alike but with the health care that marriage now brings. To-do lists that take longer now to finish half of, let alone fully accomplish. Projects that get delayed out of respect, out of exhaustion, out of businesses being literally out of business, out of fears of where the next check will come. Last month over eight hundred thousand Americans *still* filed for unemployment five months after the start of this all.

In-person events have become virtual calendar reminders and password-protected velvet ropes, prerecording performances that are then premiered on online platforms, the chat now replicating an upstairs bar turned venue in downtown Oakland as best it can. It has been inspiring to see friends contribute to and help build such local-turned-global portals for locals and new fans alike. Smart Bomb, previously a monthly showcase at the Legionnaire on Telegraph Avenue, is such a show that has helped set the standard, break isolation, and introduce heads to new music and short films. My friend Ed Ntiri's new film showcases skaters trekking through a downtown Oakland filled with new murals covering the plywood of boarded-up businesses, like artist Joonbug's murals at the Oakland Fox Theater near Oakland School of the Arts. Even the San Francisco Recreation and Parks Department has entered the live digital-streaming mix, with two live cameras documenting its expanding reserve of bison. It's oddly meditative to tune in to the animals of the Outer Lands near the Pacific at different points of the day while stuck at home, applying to jobs and avoiding a global pandemic. It allows me to briefly forget about the most recent Chevron refinery incident in Richmond polluting our skies, or the heatwave-generated local power outages that led to a failure in sewage processing, polluting the Alameda Bay instead with fifty thousand tons of waste. And still at night, to fall asleep after reading the news (again), I'll check in with the bison somewhere in the live dark night turned screen before me, noting the single-digit viewership, wondering if they can't sleep either.

Through the short films and music videos presented digitally, I can see how the parts of downtown Oakland I'm not physically encountering are changing—new condos, construction, new murals. And amid prized local businesses like Wolfman Books closing, their losses again reaffirm the need to value what's here while it's here. The *San Francisco Chronicle*'s Sunday edition has a full-page spread of the many businesses that closed this year, many after generations. It's Tops diner, Slim's, Art's Cafe, and Louis' along the Pacific Ocean, all gone in the city, let alone the Uptown, Issues bookstore, and more here in Oakland.

It's not until August that I visit San Francisco for the first time since March. Driving from Oakland to the city across the Bay Bridge is generally an annual affair, and somehow 2020 hasn't changed that. A decade ago, I had a job that took me across the bay to Redwood City, down the Peninsula, teaching after-school programs before trekking back to Oakland by way of the Dumbarton Bridge to 880 north in the East Bay, four days a week. I nearly went insane. It was antithetical to the reason for moving to the Bay Area from suburban Los Angeles. Going all city in the Bay has a cost that Los Angeles's massive highways and parallel side streets somehow alleviate, but in the Bay, even in the driver's seat, I feel like Robert Redford in *Sneakers*, kidnapped and stuffed inside a moving vehicle, listening to the sound of the bridge's concrete slabs thinking themselves into a rhythm, a crude percussion.

The city arrives and the new skyscrapers shine over the old Hills Bros. Coffee building to my right, with the new Warriors arena and subsequent China Basin and Mission Bay developments to my left. The pedestrian POV quickly takes over and I can see the old Sailors' Union of the Pacific peeking between the developments leading off Fremont Street toward the redesigned, and now COVID-affected, Transbay Transit terminal, before I drive down 101 through Potrero Hill to 280, taking the long way to Portola on the other side of Twin Peaks, to see the dentist I've had since I moved to the Bay when I was seventeen. She asks me about my canceled-turned-virtual wedding, and I extol the virtues of sharing vows with family and Alameda County staff over video-conferencing apps as she pricks my gums. I distract myself from the uncomfortable nature of this exchange, however socially and medically appropriate, by trying to remember the nearby sights and skate spots, like the big hubba I always forget off Dewey, and daydream still about how this whole neighborhood was originally a sand-dune extension of the beach that led to the base of Twin Peaks and what is now the Forest Hill MUNI, the oldest subway stop in the West, and I remember that the bar referred to as Suzy's in this book, actually called the Summer Place, recently closed in the wake of the pandemic.

It's barely noon and I don't have a job to virtually

monitor, so I drive past nearby Commodore Sloat Elementary and see the double set featured in a 1990s issue of *Thrasher*, and debate what trick teenage pro Lavar McBride did down it, before passing Laguna Honda Hospital and curving my way onto 7th Avenue to Lincoln through Golden Gate Park to the Panhandle. It's been a week or so since the news announced the landlord didn't want to negotiate with Suzy and her two sons, a family that has managed and owned bars in the city since the early 1980s. I cut up Masonic for a good view of the historic four-stair and ledges at Wallenberg before taking Bush crosstown to the bar. Climbing the steep camelbacks of concrete connecting Russian and Nob Hill, I wonder if the bar's sign is still there or whether that'd be the first to go, a change in the landscape bright as a For Sale sign. I get paranoid being around humans, albeit in cars, for the first time in months, and start debating who in which car next to me is lurking not for memory but opportunity, the future of brick and mortar discussed by colleagues at my now former contract gig as well as my projections about everyone in the city around me trying to come up on cheap property, driving in our motorized petri dishes from masked point A to sanitized point B. I illegally park on a fairly empty block and see that the sign is still there, bolted and extending across the southeast corner like a mandible claw. There are somehow tourists around despite the quasi shelter in place, and there are also enough loading-zone parking slots for me to spare a few minutes of illegal meter loitering to check in on the bar's state of affairs. As I walk across Bush Street and look east, the déjà vu hits me: familiar angles of sunlight, street, and multigenerational metropolis staring back at me again like on so many Monday nights of lush, isolated escape, a derivative Bukowski-but-make-it-hippie type of vibe that now feels aged, worn.

The Summer Place has been around since the 1990s, and a local write-up gave it a proper send-off. Local journalists are tasked now with documenting the loss as much as the conditions of this changing San Francisco. Rental rates have dropped as those with functionally remote jobs, predominantly in areas of tech or finance, have left the city to go back to their non-California home states or to new apartments and homes in the East Bay and beyond. Subsequently rents and property values are increasing in areas like Lake Tahoe and Napa, near-perennial fire season be damned.

I can't see anyone inside the bar. There won't ever be anyone inside again, except those tasked with clearing it, decades of memories assumedly inside. What remains are the XL plastic bottles of cocktail mixers sitting in boxes and scattered across the bar alongside cleaning products and binders of documents. The pinball machines are gone, as is the digital jukebox, its speakers and the neon lights proclaiming various beer brands that essentially illuminated the seating area aside from the Christmas lights always hung around the bar itself. The daylight now shines through and onto those older white walls that are exposed now, and I wonder if maybe black paneling was the wall color all these years. I turn my phone sideways and take a photo of the sign. The crack running through its center has now fully crested from bottom to top.

First Street looks like a design mock with a weak pulse and forested flattop a couple of floors above, overlooking the finished, characterless street leading to the Bay Bridge's Oakland-bound entrance. Seeing the street now without all the construction is a reminder of how construction never truly stopped during the pandemic, its sounds continuing as we sit inside. Subleases of offices downtown have increased as tech bides its time, some offering to pay their workers to move out of cities like San Francisco and take a pay cut. Rideshare apps threaten to leave California if legislation doesn't go their way, and despite 2018 legislation AB 5 classifying drivers as employees, Uber and Lyft have invested millions into the antilabor "Yes on Prop 22" campaign, while organized labor has collected amounts in the single digits. The bullies have deep pockets, and the toxic Atlantic drift moves east toward Oakland, where downtown continues to rise in glass-paned stories as much as homelessness and the inability to find full-time work.

That afternoon driving back to Oakland, I don't know that in the following weeks the headlines will announce further evidence of Russian interference in both the 2016 and forthcoming 2020 elections. They will scream the whistleblower testimony of a licensed practical nurse at the ICE Irwin County Detention Center in Georgia, detailing forced medical procedures like hysterectomies on detained migrant women—the latest example of a sterilization campaign against women of color in America. They will announce the death of Supreme Court Justice Ruth Bader Ginsburg, the last chip of democracy to fall for so many of the vile politicians waiting for opportunism to strike in their favor, again, betting on the muse that is the complacency and miseducation of the American people. But whatever next week, month, year brings or the election results determine, my mind is stuck on Wednesday, September 9, 2020: the day California's skies turned a black orange from wildfires, like oxygen imploded and turned its back, never to return.

Two weeks later, I drive back to the city again, the same drive from Portola to 7th Avenue to the Panhandle and across town. I pull over on the bodega side for a quick unpaid meter risk to get a glimpse of the bar and, really, the cracked lightning bolt of a sign hanging over the corner and see that it's still there. The windows are boarded up now, the bar maybe behind there, maybe not. The front door's reflection now is as opaque as this orange, hazardous sky haunting Northern California, Oregon, Washington, and the entirety of the West Coast, and in either vision, I am the fool for assuming that such habitual, repeated staring could generate a recognizable reflection.

Acknowledgments

It should be noted that the memorial tombstone in Fresno referenced in the title essay—honoring the victims of all thirty-two passengers killed in the 1948 plane crash at Los Gatos Canyon—was led by the efforts of Tim Z. Hernandez and Carlos Rascon, along with many local volunteers. Additionally, I thank the staff and volunteers of the California landmarks and businesses cited in this book and the many analog and digital preservationists of California's histories.

These words and the opportunity to create a collection of essays would not have been possible without the dedication, support, and editorial guidance of Mensah Demary. From the slush pile to publication, thank you for seeing this work and simply changing my life.

Thank you to Yuka Igarashi for acquiring this manuscript during her tenure at Soft Skull Press. Thank you to the Soft Skull, Catapult, and Counterpoint staff for their thoughtful support. Thank you to Monika Woods for the early manuscript feedback. Melissa Valentine, Lauren Whitehead, Mariama Lockington, Kyle Beachy, sam sax, Nina Renata Aron—thank you for your blurbs and early support.

Thank you to everyone in the Bay Area literary and performing arts communities who have supported me from 2003 to the present, including but not limited to: Pro Arts Gallery and Commons, The Place for Writers at Mills College, Youth Speaks, Intersection for the Arts, Life Is Living Festival, New Life Quarterly / Wolfman Books, Reveal, and the many artists, organizers, educators, and friends who make it happen.

Reluctantly, thank you to Camilo Alejandro Sánchez.

"A writer is someone who writes"—thank you, Saul Landau. You are missed.

Thank you, Matt Malkin. Thank you to the Farns— worth family and to Meghann Farnsworth, for reading every draft and being my best friend.

Thank you to Esteban Gomez, mi primo. Thank you to the extended Gomez and Vadi family trees.

To my family—José Miguel, Delfina, and Marissa Vadi—I hope these words are a testament to the ganas you and Antonio Gomez encouraged me to have. Know you are loved.

JOSÉ VADI is an award-winning essayist, poet, playwright, and film producer. Vadi received the San Francisco Foundation's Shenson Performing Arts Award for his debut play, *a eulogy for three*, produced by Marc Bamuthi Joseph's Living Word Project. He is the author of *SoMa Lurk*, a collection of photos and poems published by Project Kalahati / Pro Arts Commons. His work has been featured by the *PBS NewsHour*, the *San Francisco Chronicle*, and *The Daily Beast*, while his writing has appeared in *Catapult*, *McSweeney's*, *New Life Quarterly*, *The Los Angeles Review of Books*, SFMOMA's *Open Space*, and *Pop-Up Magazine*.